3

rain
train
strain
restrain
restraints

Sequential Spelling

By Don McCabe

1 Printing   Year 11

Publisher's Cataloging in Publication Data

McCabe, Donald J., *Sequential Spelling*.—Rev. ed., Arlington Heights, IL: *Wave 3 Learning*, Inc. c2011.
        Volume 3 of a 7 Volume series.

1. Spelling—Miscellanea. 2. Reading—Miscellanea. 3. Curriculum—Miscellanea 4. Literacy and Tutor Reference Tool.
Library of Congress Subject Headings: Spelling, Curriculum
Library of Congress Classification Number: LB1050.2F79
Library of Congress Card Number: To be determined
Dewey Decimal Classification Number 428.4
ISBN: 9781935943105

About *Sequential Spelling*

Sequential Spelling is a research-based system rooted in the classic Orton-Gillingham approach to learning. Developed by Don McCabe, Executive Director of the AVKO Educational Research Foundation, the curriculum provides multi-sensory spelling instruction. The student learns sets of words that share patterns of spelling rather than thematically related lists of words. This methodology enables the student with a learning difference to focus on learning a given sequence of letters, how they sound, and the words they appear in.

About this Edition

This edition of the *Sequential Spelling* series has been expanded. Each level now has a coordinating student workbook, complete with a daily "Using Your Words" activity. The teaching methodology described in the earlier edition has remained the same; however, the teacher guide now includes an answer key. We have also replaced some of the words used in the original edition with other words from *The Patterns of English Spelling* (a related product available from *Wave 3 Learning*).

Marjorie Lock, Editor
Wave 3 Learning
January 2011

Table of Contents

To the Teacher

<u>OVERVIEW</u>

Sequential Spelling uses word families or word patterns as its teaching method. The student learns the phonics sounds necessary for decoding words while learning to spell. For example, if you can teach the word **at** you can also teach:

bat	bats	batted	batting		
cat	cats				
scat	scats				
flat	flats	flatted	flatting		
pat	pats	patted	patting		
spat	spats				
mat	mats	matted	matting		
rat	rats	ratted	ratting		
batter	batters	battered	battering	battery	batteries
flatter	flatters	flattered	flattering	flattery	
matter	matters	mattered	mattering		
battle	battles	battled	battling		
cattle					
rattle	rattles	rattled	rattling		

similarly, from the word **act** you can build:

act	acts	acted	acting	active	action
fact	facts				
tract	tracts	traction			
attract	attracts	attracted	attracting	attractive	attraction
distract	distracts	distracted	distracting	distraction	
extract	extracts	extracted	extracting	extractive	extraction
subtract	subtracts	subtracted	subtracting	subtraction	
contract	contracts	contracted	contracting	contraction	

Spelling rules are not specifically taught in this curriculum. Rather, they are learned as part of the daily spelling lesson. A description of some of the more frequently used spelling rules is included at the end of this Guide.

<u>HALLMARKS OF *SEQUENTIAL SPELLING*</u>

- daily spelling tests with immediate feedback
- multi-sensory teaching (audio, visual, kinesthetic and oral) of spelling patterns
- base words are introduced first, then the endings for them (-s, -ed, -ing) on subsequent days.
- 180 lessons per level
- levels are not matched to grade level. Most students should begin at level 1.

Teaching the Lessons

MATERIALS NEEDED:

- Easel or dry erase board
- Different colored markers
- Student Response Book or notebook paper
- Teacher's guide

LESSON TIME:

15-20 minutes

LESSON PREPARATION:

Review the words for the spelling test before beginning the lesson to familiarize yourself with tricky spellings, homophones, etc.

Have students open their workbooks and find the page for the day's lesson. If they are using notebook paper for the spelling test, use one sheet per lesson.

LESSON FORMAT:

Each day will consist of a spelling test. Rather than teaching the spelling of each word, teachers should concentrate on teaching the basic sounds of each word. For example, when you are teaching the word family **–ange** *(range, ranges, arrange, arranges, arrangement, arrangements)* what is important is the teaching of the **–ange** ending, the plural ending and the **–ment** suffix as well as the initial consonant sounds and consonant blends.

Teaching Methodology
- Give each word separately.
- Say the word. Give it in a sentence.
- Let the student/s attempt the spelling.
- Give the correct spelling. Let each student correct their own spelling. Then give the next word.

Teaching Steps
Using contrasting marker colors will allow your students to more easily recognize the word patterns in each word. For example: when you give the correct spelling of **spinning** write the base **–in** in your base word color. Then, *"double the **n** and add **ing** to get **inning**."* Add **p** and **s** in a contrasting color to get **spinning.**

NOTE: The most common mistake made in teaching *Sequential Spelling* is to give the entire test and then correct it. Students must self correct after each word, not at the end of the test.

Extra practice with homophone lists

At the bottom of each page are lists of homophones (words which sound exactly alike but have different meanings as well as spellings). You may want to include some practice of these concepts in your spelling lessons. Here are a few ideas for teaching homophones:

Homophone Pictionary – Give your student a card with the homophone pair and have them draw pictures of each. The other students can guess the homophones.

Silly Sentences – Give your students a list of homophone pairs and have them come up with silly sentences using the homophone pair.

Homophone Old Maid – Make about twenty pairs of cards with a homophone written on them. Include an "old maid" card as well. Deal the cards as evenly as possible. Then play "Old Maid." When there is a match, have the student show both cards and define EACH word in the homophone pair or use them correctly in a sentence.

ABC Homophone - Have your students come up with twenty-six homophone pairs, one for each letter of the alphabet.

Student Book

The student workbook (available separately from *Wave 3 Learning* Wave3Learning.com) has a "Using Your Words" section after each lesson. Students are given brief assignments to stretch their use of the words they have just learned. Four *Story Starter* pages are also included at the back of the book for use as creative writing exercises. The answer key for the student workbook is in this teacher edition. After teaching the day's lesson, you can choose to have your student complete the "Using Your Words" section of their workbook, extend the lesson as described below or move on to another subject.

PROGRESS EVALUATION

Evaluation tests are provided after the 40th, 80th, 120th, 160th and 180th lessons. If you choose to create other tests for grading purposes, they should be given at a separate time and students should be graded on their learning of the spelling of the sounds—not the words.

Administering the Evaluation Tests

Read the tests aloud to your students and ask them to complete the word in the sentence. Initial consonants and blends are given – only the spelling pattern used is tested.

ABOUT THE TEACHER TEXT

Notations

* asterisks remind the teacher that the word has a homophone (same pronunciation, different spelling) or heteronym (same spelling, different word and different pronunciation), or does not follow the normal pattern. For example, gyp ** should logically be spelled "jip." Similarly, the word proper ** should logically be spelled "propper" just like hopper, and copper, and stopper, but it is not. Homophones and homographs are listed for your convenience so that you make sure to use the word correctly in a sentence, like "billed. We were billed for extra carpeting. billed" or "build. We will build our house on a hill. build"

Abbreviations   Am = American spelling   Br = British spelling

Words in Bold Print

These are the most commonly used words and the most important to learn. Some words (like doesn't) don't follow regular word patterns and are repeated many times throughout the series. So, you do not have to use all the words in each word list, but please make sure you cover all the words in bold print. At the end of this curriculum, your students should be able to spell the most common words and have learned the most common patterns that occur in words.

Student Handwriting Expectations

Since the students correct their own spelling, they should be expected to write clearly and legibly. The daily tests can and should be used for handwriting practice because the patterns, being repetitive, can be a help in developing legible handwriting. As the teacher, you should set clear standards for acceptable handwriting on these spelling tests.

CUSTOMIZING *SEQUENTIAL SPELLING* FOR YOUR STUDENT

Change the Words on the Tests

You may decide you want to add, change or delete some words on each day's spelling list. Great! If you would prefer to start with a different word family, feel free. *Sequential Spelling* lists most of the words in each family, but not all. We have a supplemental resource, *The Patterns of English Spelling*, which has lists of all the word family patterns used in the series. It is available for purchase from www.wave3learning.com.

Give the Test Again

If you decide to give the test again, allow at least two hours between re-tests. We also recommend that the absolute maximum number of times that *Sequential Spelling* tests be given each day is four times.

Increase/Decrease the Pace

Increase the time spent each day on spelling. You could try going through four days of *Sequential Spelling* 1 every day until it is finished and then move through four days of *Sequential Spelling* 2 every day, and continue on through four levels of *Sequential Spelling* in six months.

Lets get started!

	1st day	2nd day	3rd day	4th day
1.	**gas**	gasses	gassed	gassing
2.	gasoline	gasoline	gassy	gasoline
3.	* alas	alas	sassafras	sassafras
4.	* a lass	lasses	lassie	lassies
5.	**glass**	**glasses**	classy	classiest
6.	class	classes	classed	classing
7.	grass	grasses	passer	passers
8.	pass	passes	* **passed**	passing
9.	trespass	trespasses	trespassed	trespassers
10.	surpass	surpasses	surpassed	surpassing
11.	mass	masses	* massed	massing
12.	** bass	overpass	bluegrass	spyglass
13.	**brass**	underpass	bypass	eyeglasses
14.	**yes**	less	lest	lesser
15.	mess	messes	messed	messing
16.	**guess**	**guesses**	* **guessed**	guessing
17.	**dress**	dresses	dressed	**dressing**
18.	undress	undressed	* less	**unless**
19.	process	processed	processing	processed
20.	**success**	successes	**successful**	successfully
21.	bless	* **blessed**	successive	succession
22.	confess	confessed	confessing	confession
23.	profess	professed	professor	profession
24.	press	presses	pressed	pressing
25.	depress	depressed	depressing	depression

* **Homophones:**

alas/a lass	Alas, it was a lass and not a lad that won the tournament.
passed/past	When we passed through Chicago, it was way past midnight.
massed/mast	The men in Moby Dick were massed around the mast of the ship.
blessed/blest	We were blessed (or blest) as the case may be.
guessed/guest	The guest guessed correctly to wait for the host to begin eating.

* **Heteronyms**:

bass ("bass")/bass ("BAY'ss") We went fishing for bass. Jack sang bass.

See the complete -ass family on p. 156 in *The Patterns of English Spelling* (TPES); the -aw, p. 319; the –es (ess) p. 157.

	5th day	6th day	7th day	8th day
1.	impress	**impressed**	impressive	impression
2.	compress	compresses	compressing	compression
3.	decompress	decompressed	decompresses	decompression
4.	oppress	oppressed	oppressive	oppression
5.	express	expressed	expressive	expression
6.	**stress**	stressed	stresses	stressing
7.	distress	excess	excessive	lesson
8.	assess	assessed	assessment	assessor
9.	nevertheless	watercress	chess	housedress
10.	bench-press	access	redress	egress
11.	**possess**	possessed	possessive	possession
12.	** made **progress**	hard-pressed	duress	Miss Hess
13.	** to progress	progressed	progressive	progression
14.	**kiss**	**kisses**	**kissed**	kissing
15.	**miss**	misses	* **missed**	missing
16.	dismiss	dismisses	dismissed	dismissal
17.	* amiss	hit-and-miss	Swiss	bliss
18.	a miss	hiss	hissed	hissing
19.	**bus**	buses	* bused	busing
20.	buss[1]	busses	bussed	bussing
21.	**plus**	thus	beauty	beautiful
22.	**fuss**	fusses	fussed	fussing
23.	cuss	cusses	cussed	cussing
24.	**discuss**	**discusses**	**discussed**	discussion
25.	truss	trusses	trussed	focus

* **Homophones**:

missed/mist	When the mayor of London visited Arizona, he said he missed the mist.
bussed/bust/bused	The bust of Shakespeare was bused (or bussed) from school to school.
amiss/a miss	Something's amiss here. The announcer said "swing and a miss! Strike three!"

** **Heteronyms**:

progress n. ("PRAH gress")/progress v. ("proh GRESS")

See the complete -iss family on p. 158 in *The Patterns of English Spelling* (TPES); the -uss, p. 160; the -us, p. 160.

[1]The word buss means to kiss.

Sequential Spelling Level 3 - Teacher's Guide

	9th day	10th day	11th day	12th day
1.	**best**	pest	west	* blest
2.	**nest**	nests	nested	nesting
3.	**test**	tests	tested	testing
4.	detest	detests	detested	detesting
5.	protest	protests	protested	protesting
6.	attest[1]	attests	attested	attesting
7.	**rest**	rests	rested	resting
8.	arrest	arrests	arrested	arresting
9.	vest	vests	zest	zestful
10.	invest	invests	invested	investment
11.	**suggest**	suggests	suggested	**suggestion**
12.	digest	digests	digested	digestion
13.	congest	congested	congestive	congestion
14.	infest	infested	one* **guest**	two guests
15.	eve	eves	**even**	**evening**
16.	peeve	peeves	peeved	pet peeves
17.	**sleeve**	sleeves	sleeveless	shirtsleeves
18.	**seven**	sevens	seventy	seventy-seven
19.	**eleven**	elevens	heaven	heavens
20.	leaven	leavens	leavened	unleavened
21.	event	events	eventful	eventually
22.	**ever**	whatever	whatsoever	wherever
23.	lever	clever	whenever	whoever
24.	whoever	however	**forever**	**beautiful**
25.	sever	severed	severing	**several**

* Homophones:

blest/blessed   They were blest (or blessed) as the case may be.

guest/guessed   You guessed right. The speaker was my guest.

See the complete -est family on p. 234 in *The Patterns of English Spelling* (TPES); the -eve, p. 324; the -even, p. 339; the -ever, 669.

[1]The test in attest is similar to that in testimony, testify, and testament.

	13th day	14th day	15th day	16th day
1.	thief	thieves	thief	thieving
2.	**belief**	believes	beliefs	believing
3.	**brief**	briefs	briefed	briefly
4.	debrief	debriefs	debriefed	debriefing
5.	**chief**	chiefs	chiefly	beauties
6.	kerchief	kerchiefs	neckerchief	neckerchiefs
7.	handkerchief	handkerchiefs	**mischief**	**mischievous**
8.	**relief**	relieves	relieving	relief
9.	**grief**	grieves	grieving	briefcase
10.	achieve	achieves	achieving	achievement
11.	**leave**	leaf	leaves	**leaving**
12.	weave	weaves	weaving	deceit
13.	* eave	eaves	receipt	receipts
14.	heave	heaves	heaved	heaving
15.	**receive**	**receives**	**receiving**	**reception**
16.	deceive	deceives	deceiving	deception
17.	perceive	perceives	perceived	perception
18.	conceive	conceived	inconceivable	conception
19.	preconceive	preconceived	misconceived	preconception
20.	jazz	jazzes	jazzed	jazzing
21.	razz	razzes	razzed	razzing
22.	razzmatazz	isn't	wasn't	hasn't
23.	quiz	quizzes	quizzed	quizzing
24.	whiz	whizzes	whizzed	whizzing
25.	fizz	fizzes	fizzed	fizzing

* **Homophones**:

eve/eave   Did Eve stand under the eave?

See the complete -ief family on p. 406 in *The Patterns of English Spelling* (TPES); the -ieve, p. 441; the -ceive, p. 441; the -azz, p. 136; the -izz, p. 138.

Sequential Spelling Level 3 - Teacher's Guide

	17th day	18th day	19th day	20th day
1.	fuzz	fuzzy	fuzzier	fuzziest
2.	buzz	buzzes	buzzed	buzzing
3.	buzzer	buzzers	buzzard	buzzards
4.	**puzzle**	puzzles	puzzled	puzzling
5.	muzzle	muzzles	muzzled	muzzling
6.	**does**	doesn't	was	wasn't
7.	**rifle**	rifles	rifled	rifling
8.	trifle	trifles	trifled	trifling
9.	stifle	stifles	stifled	stifling
10.	**stiff**	stiffs	stiffer	stiffest
11.	sniff	sniffs	sniffed	sniffing
12.	cliff	cliffs	skiff	skiffs
13.	whiff	whiffs	whiffed	whiffing
14.	**sheriff**	sheriffs	the sheriff's badge	sheriff
15.	tariff	tariffs	mastiff	mastiffs
16.	tiff	tiffs	riff	miff
17.	plaintiff	plaintiffs	mischief	handkerchief
18.	**puff**	puffs	puffed	puffing
19.	**stuff**	stuffs	**stuffed**	**stuffing**
20.	* **ruff**	ruffs	ruffed	ruffing
21.	cuff	**cuffs**	cuffed	cuffing
22.	handcuff	handcuffs	handcuffed	handcuffing
23.	scuff	scuffs	**scuffed**	scuffing
24.	**bluff**	bluffs	**bluffed**	**bluffing**
25.	**suffer**	**suffers**	**suffered**	**suffering**

* **Homophones**:

ruff/rough   It can be rough to wear a scratchy ruff.

See the complete -uzz family on p. 140 in *The Patterns of English Spelling* (TPES); the -ifle, p. 612; the -iff, p. 143; the -uff, p. 145.

	21st day	22nd day	23rd day	24th day
1.	* **air**	airs	aired	airing
2.	* **pair**	pairs	paired	pairing
3.	**chair**	chairs	chaired	chairing
4.	* **hair**	hairs	red-haired	fair-haired
5.	* **fair**	fairs	**unfair**	unfairly
6.	repair	repairs	**repaired**	repairing
7.	impair	impairs	impaired	impairment
8.	despair	despairs	despaired	despairing
9.	airport	airline	airsick	hairball
10.	**stairs**	stairway	stair steps	upstairs
11.	* **wear**	wears	wore/worn	wearing
12.	**swear**	swears	swore/sworn	swearing
13.	* (**) **tear**	tears	tore/torn	tearing
14.	* **pear**	pears	sportswear	underwear
15.	* **bear**	bears	bore/borne	bearing
16.	* **heir**	heirs	heirloom	heiress
17.	* their * heir	It was * theirs.	*Your * heir	* It's * theirs.
18.	**care**	cares	cared	caring
19.	**scare**	scares	**scared**	scaring
20.	dare	dares	dared	daring
21.	* bare	* bares	* bared	* baring
22.	**stare**	* **stares**	stared	staring
23.	**share**	shares	shared	sharing
24.	**spare**	spares	spared	sparing
25.	**square**	squares	squared	squaring

* **Homophones**:

fair/fare	What do you call a just ticket price? A fair fare.
air/heir	The heir to the throne breathes rare air.
they're/their/there	They're going to build their house over there.
there's/theirs	There's something special about everything that is theirs.
you're/your/yore	You're going to discover your ancestors lived in the days of yore.
it's/its	It's too bad the dog couldn't catch its tail.
pear/pair	What do you call a couple of Bartletts? A pear pair.
hare/hair	What do you call rabbit fur? Hare hair.
ware/wear	What do you call clothing for sale? Wear ware.
bare/bear	What do you call a naked grizzlie? A bare bear.
tare/tear	What do you call the weight of a rip? The tare tear.

* **Heteronyms**:

tear "TEER"/tear "TAY'r"   We shed a tear or two when we saw how big a tear there was in the tent.

See the complete -air family on p. 530 in *The Patterns of English Spelling*; the -ear, p. 530; the –eir p.530; the -are p. 523.

	25th day	26th day	27th day	28th day
1.	* **fare**	fares	fared	faring
2.	welfare	airfare	warfare	bus fare
3.	* **pare**	pares	pared	paring
4.	**prepare**	prepares	prepared	preparing
5.	**compare**	compares	compared	comparing
6.	glare	glares	glared	glaring
7.	snare	snares	snared	snaring
8.	* **ware**	wares	hardware	software
9.	silverware	cookware	aware	unaware
10.	* **flare**	flares	flared	flaring
11.	* **mare**	* mares	rare	rarely
12.	* **beware**	Delaware	bareback	barefoot
13.	scarce	scarcely	scarce	scarcely
14.	**word**	words	worded	wording
15.	reword	reworded	password	* foreword
16.	**work**	works	worked	working
17.	workers	workable	workbench	workbook
18.	* **world**	worlds	worldly	world-wide
19.	worm	worms	wormed	worming
20.	silkworm	wormy	wormhole	tapeworm
21.	**worry**	worries	worried	worrying
22.	worrywart	worrisome	worse	worst
23.	worship	worships	worshipped	worshipping
24.	**worth**	worthless	worthwhile	worthiness
25.	patchwork	fireworks	woodworking	worshipper

* Homophones:

fair/fare	Honest prices for travel would be fair fare.
pair/pear/pare	Two is a pair. A pear is a fruit. You can pare an apple or a potato.
wear/ware	What do you call clothing? Wear ware.
flare/flair	What do you call a penchant for lighting up the skies? A flare flair.
forward/foreword	What do you call a fresh preface? A forward foreword.

See the complete -are family on p. 523 in *The Patterns of English Spelling* (TPES); the -arce, p. 509; the -wor, p. 503.

	29th day	30th day	31st day	32nd day
1.	**large**	largely	larger	largest
2.	**charge**	charges	charged	charging
3.	recharge	recharged	charger	enlarger
4.	enlarge	enlarged	enlargement	enlarging
5.	discharge	discharged	discharging	surcharge
6.	overcharge	undercharge	barge	barges
7.	Marge	margin	marginal	marginally
8.	**soup**	soups	soupy	soups
9.	**group**	groups	grouped	trouping
10.	regroup	regroups	regrouped	regrouping
11.	recoup	recoups	recouped	recouping
12.	coup	coups	coupon	croup
13.	**rip**	rips	**ripped**	ripping
14.	**trip**	trips	**tripped**	tripping
15.	**strip**	strips	stripped	stripping
16.	grip	grips	gripped	gripping
17.	**drip**	drips	dripped	dripping
18.	**tip**	tips	tipped	tipping
19.	**lip**	lips	lipped	lipping
20.	**slip**	slips	slipped	**slippers**
21.	clip	clips	clipped	clippers
22.	flip	flips	flipped	flipping
23.	**dip**	dips	dipped	dipper
24.	sip	snips	sipped	snipping
25.	**whip**	whips	**whipped**	**whipping**

See the complete -arge family on p. 507 in *The Patterns of English Spelling* (TPES); the -ip, p. 128.

	33rd day	34th day	35th day	36th day
1.	skip	skips	skipped	skipper
2.	**chip**	**chips**	chipped	chipping
3.	ship	ships	shipped	shipping
4.	gyp	gyps	gypped	gypping
5.	gypsy	gypsies	turnips	tightlipped
6.	tulip	* **tulips**	horsewhip	horsewhipped
7.	worship	worships	* worshipped	* worshipping
8.	zip	unzipped	zipper	zippers
9.	gossip[1]	gossips	gossiping	gossiping
10.	battleship	parsnips	* worshiped	* worshiping
11.	partnership	spaceship	hardship	friendship
12.	relationship	fingertips	* worshipers	* worshippers
13.	**top**	topped	topping	proper
14.	**stopped**	stopping	stopper	properly
15.	popped	popping	popper	property
16.	slop	slops	slopped	sloppy
17.	cops	**copper**	chopping	chopper
18.	**hop**	hops	**hopped**	**hopping**
19.	mop	mops	mopped	mopping
20.	drop	drops	dropped	dropping
21.	crop	crops	proper[1]	**improper**
22.	prop	props	propped	propping
23.	**copy**[1]	**copies**	**copied**	**copying**
24.	**photocopy**	**photocopies**	**copier**	**copiers**
25.	**miscopy**	**miscopies**	**miscopied**	**miscopying**

* Homophones:

worshipped/worshiped	Most of us worshipped; some of us worshiped.
worshipping/worshiping	Most of us were worshipping; some of us were worshiping.
worshippers/worshipers	Most of us were worshippers; some of us were worshipers.

See the complete -ip family on p. 128 in *The Patterns of English Spelling* (TPES); the -op, p. 129.

---

[1]Words such as *gossip*, *proper*, and *copy* differ from other -ip and -op words in the way suffixes are added. Since each base cannot be reduced to one syllable the letter p does not double when adding a suffix such as er, ed or ing. However, the p in the word worship can be doubled. Have your students be consistent..

	37th day	38th day	39th day	40th day
1.	whopper	floppy	poppy	poppies
2.	nonstop	raindrops	blacktop	floppies
3.	eavesdrop	lollipops	pork chops	window-shopping
4.	ash	ashes	cashier	cashiers
5.	**cash**	cashes	cashed	cashing
6.	**trash**	trashes	trashed	trashing
7.	thrash	thrashes	thrashed	thrashing
8.	lash	clashes	flashed	dashing
9.	splash	splashes	splashed	splashing
10.	mash	smashes	mashed	smashing
11.	stash	stashes	stashed	hashing
12.	**wash**[1]	**washes**	**washed**	**washing**
13.	**fashion**[2]	fashions	old-fashioned	old-fashioned
14.	washer	washers	Washington	wishy-washy
15.	**wish**	**wishes**	wished	wishing
16.	**dish**	**dishes**	dished	dishing
17.	fish	fished	fishing	fisherman
18.	swish	swished	swishing	goldfish
19.	shellfish	jellyfish	catfish	starfish
20.	**selfish**	selfishly	unselfish	unselfishly
21.	**rush**	rushes	**rushed**	rushing
22.	**brush**	**brushes**	brushed	brushing
23.	crush	crushes	**crushed**	crushing
24.	**blush**	blushed	**blushing**	crusher
25.	flush	gushes	hushed	flushing

See the complete -ash family on p. 209 in *The Patterns of English Spelling* (TPES); the -ish, p. 210; the -ush, p. 211.

[1] W-control over the letter A gives the "AH" sound. See p. 504 in *The Patterns of English Spelling* (TPES)

[2] SHI = "SH;" ON = "UN." The "AA - SHUN" sound can be spelled three ways: -a + ti + on as in ration, -a + ssi + on as in passion. Compare the spelling of the "shun" sound in fashion (shion) to the spelling of the "shun" sound in cushion (shion) in the next set of lessons.

Evaluation Test #1 (After 40 Days)

		Pattern being tested	Lesson word is in
1.	Has that suspect conf**essed** to the murder yet?	essed	2
2.	I hope we don't have another depr**ession**.	ession	4
3.	I have not dism**issed** this class yet.	issed	7
4.	We'll have a group disc**ussion** tomorrow.	ussion	8
5.	What was that group prot**esting** over?	esting	12
6.	I would like to make a sugg**estion**.	estion	12
7.	The policeman caught the th**ief** red-handed.	ief	13
8.	We bel**ieve*** you.	ieve	14
9.	I love going to wedding re**ceptions***.	ceptions	16
10.	I am really p**uzzled** by your reaction.	uzzled	19
11.	There is too much s**uffering** in this world.	uffering	20
12.	We should have our roof rep**aired** before it leaks.	aired	23
13.	I wish you would stop st**aring** at me.	aring	24
14.	We were prep**ared** for almost any emergency.	ared	27
15.	I wish you would stop comp**aring** me to my sister.	aring	28
16.	Do you know the pass**wor**d?	wor	27
17.	We were really **wor**ried about you.	wor	27
18.	Yes, they called a ch**arging** foul on Michael Jordan.	arging	32
19.	I can remember the last time I got a wh**ipping**.	ipping	32
20.	My cousin sk**ipped** the fourth grade.	ipped	35

*These words were never given, but other forms of these words were used.

	41st day	42nd day	43rd day	44th day
1.	**push**	pushes	pushed	pushing
2.	**bush**	**bushes**	bushed	bushing
3.	ambush	ambushes	ambushed	ambushing
4.	bushel	bushels	pincushion	pincushions
5.	cushion	cushions	cushioned	cushioning
6.	**door**	doors	beautiful	beautifully
7.	**floor**	floors	floored	flooring
8.	subfloor	subfloors	subflooring	beauties
9.	outdoor	outdoors	indoor	indoors
10.	next-door	trapdoor	out-of-doors	doorknob
11.	doormat	door prize	doorway	doorstop
12.	doorstep	doorman	doorbell	poorhouse
13.	* **poor**	poorly	poorer	poorest
14.	moor	moors	moored	mooring
15.	boor	boors	a Moor	Thomas Moore
16.	* **four**	fours	fourth	4th
17.	two-by-four	2x4	downpour	pouring
18.	* **pour**	pours	poured	outpouring
19.	* **your**	yours	yourself	yourselves
20.	* **or**	* for	forever	forehead
21.	abhor	abhors	abhorred	abhorring
22.	decor	condor	picador	toreador
23.	counselor	matador	cuspidor	corridor
24.	metaphor	ambassador	favor	nor
25.	anchor	anchors	anchored	anchoring

* Homophones:

or/ore/oar	A paddle is a type of oar. Steel is made from iron ore. Believe it or not.
your/yore/you're	Your story was based on the days of yore. You're kidding, aren't you?
four/fore/for	The four boys yelled, "Fore" just for kicks.
pour/pore	Please, pour me a drink. If a pore gets clogged you can get a pimple.

See the complete -ush family on p. 211 in *The Patterns of English Spelling* (TPES); the -oor, p. 532; the -our, p. 532; the -or, p. 516.

	45th day	46th day	47th day	48th day
1.	* **our**	ours	ourselves	**although**
2.	**hour**	hours	**through**	**though**
3.	* **flour**	* **flours**	**thorough**	**thoroughly**
4.	**sour**	sours	soured	souring
5.	scour	scours	scoured	scouring
6.	devour	devours	devoured	devouring
7.	**flower**	* **flowers**	flowered	flowering
8.	**power**	powers	powered	powering
9.	overpower	overpowers	overpowered	overpowering
10.	tower	towers	towered	towering
11.	**shower**	showers	showered	showering
12.	**horn**	horns	horned	horning
13.	**corn**	corns	corny	corniest
14.	scorn	scorns	scorned	scorning
15.	adorn	adorns	adorned	adorning
16.	* **morn**	* **morning**	morn	* **morning**
17.	* **mourn**	mourns	mourned	* **mourning**
18.	**warn**[1]	warns	warned	**warning**
19.	acorn	acorns	popcorn	freeborn
20.	inborn	shorn	adorn	outworn
21.	shopworn	well-worn	forlorn	unicorn
22.	**born**	newborn	unborn	torn
23.	thorn	foghorn	**although**	**through**
24.	beauty	beauties	**beautiful**	beautifully
25.	beautify	beautifies	beautified	beautifying

* Homophones:

our/are	You are in our house. (Midwestern American Dialect and other dialects)
our/hour	In one hour we can be in our house. (Standard dialects)
flower/flour	A bread of roses would be made from flower flour.
morning/mourning	What do you call crying early in the day? Morning mourning.

See the complete -our family on p. 532 in *The Patterns of English Spelling* (TPES); the -ower, p. 532; the -orn, pp. 517.

---

[1] See p. 502 in *The Patterns of English Spelling* for the W- and -R controls and their WAR over the letter A.

	49th day	50th day	51st day	52nd day
1.	**port**	ports	portable	portage
2.	import	imports	imported	importing
3.	export	exports	exported	exporting
4.	transport	transports	transported	transportation
5.	**report**	reports	reported	reporters
6.	deport	deported	deporting	deportation
7.	**support**	supports	supported	supportive
8.	sort	sorts	sorted	sorting
9.	**short**	shorts	shortage	shortages
10.	snort	snorts	snorted	snorting
11.	**sport**	sports	sportswear	life-support
12.	passport	passports	**although**	extorting
13.	extort	extorts	extorted	extortion
14.	abort	aborts	aborted	abortion
15.	escort	escorts	escorted	escorting
16.	**fort**	forts	carport	airport
17.	distort	distorts	distorted	distortion
18.	shortcake	shortsighted	shortcut	shortbread
19.	noun	nouns	announce	announcer
20.	pronoun	pronouns	pronounce	pronounced
21.	**count**	counts	counted	counting
22.	account	accounts	accounted	accounting
23.	**amount**	amounts	amounted	amounting
24.	**discount**	discounts	discounted	**county**
25.	mount	dismount	**mountain**	counties

See the complete -ort family on p. 519 in *The Patterns of English Spelling* (TPES); the -oun, p. 421; the -ounce, p. 257; the -ount, p. 252.

Sequential Spelling Level 3 - Teacher's Guide

	53rd day	54th day	55th day	56th day
1.	**ounce**	ounces	bouncer	bouncers
2.	**bounce**	bounces	bounced	bouncing
3.	pounce	pounces	pounced	pouncing
4.	trounce	trounces	trounced	trouncing
5.	flounce	flounces	flounced	flouncing
6.	announce	announcing	announcer	**although**
7.	pronounce	pronouncing	pronounced	pronunciation[7]
8.	mispronounce	mispronounced	mispronounced	mispronunciation
9.	denounce	denounced	denouncing	denunciation
10.	renounce	renounced	renouncing	renunciation
11.	**down**	**downs**	downed	downing
12.	crown	crowns	crowned	crowning
13.	**frown**	frowns	frowned	frowning
14.	**brown**	browns	brownie	brownies
15.	**drown**	drowns	drowned	drowning
16.	**clown**	clowns	clowned	clowning
17.	**town**	**towns**	downtown	township
18.	sundown	knockdown	spelldown	touchdowns
19.	touchdown	upside down	letdown	showdown
20.	**rich**	riches	richer	richest
21.	richly	** Richard	* which	**which**
22.	**sandwich**	sandwiches	sandwiched	sandwiching
23.	**mile**	miles	miler	mileage
24.	**smile**	smiles	smiled	**smiling**
25.	**pile**	piles	piled	piling

* **Homonyms**:

which/witch   Which of the witch costumes will you wear for Halloween?

** **Heteronyms**:

Richard ("RICH ur'd")/ Richard ("ree SHAH'r-d")

Many English-speaking people are descended from the French. Consequently, names may either keep the French pronunciation or take on an English pronunciation. When the name Richard is a last name coupled with a common French name such as Pierre, Maurice ("moh'r REE'ss"), etc., it is usually pronounced "ree SHAH'r-d." In Parisian French the ending /d/ is dropped.

See the complete -ounce family on p. 257 in *The Patterns of English Spelling* (TPES); the -own, p. 421; the -ich, 203; the -ile, p. 330.

[7]Note the change of spelling when adding the tion ending to words with ounce.

	57th day	58th day	59th day	60th day
1.	**while**	awhile	**meanwhile**	worthwhile
2.	**file**	files	filed	**filing**
3.	compile	compiles	compiling	compilation
4.	unpile	unpiles	unpiled	unpiling
5.	defile	defiles	defiled	defiling
6.	stockpile	stockpiles	stockpiled	stockpiling
7.	reconcile	reconciles	reconciled	reconciliation
8.	**tile**	tiles	tiled	tiling
9.	rile	riles	riled	sterile
10.	exile	exiles	exiled	exiling
11.	* **style**	styles	styled	styling
12.	* **stile**	stiles	turnstile	turnstiles
13.	crocodile	profile	high profile	low profile
14.	lifestyle	lifestyles	senile	juvenile
15.	reptile	projectile	vile	wile
16.	* **hole**	holes	holed	holing
17.	* **whole**	wholesale	* **wholly**	* **holy**
18.	* **pole**	poles	poled	poling
19.	one ** **console**	two ** **consoles**	foxhole	posthole
20.	** **console**	consoles	consoled	consoling
21.	parole	dole	doled	consolation
22.	pigeonhole	pigeonholes	pigeonholed	pigeonholing
23.	keyhole	mole	oriole	loophole
24.	porthole	tadpole	mink stole	* **sole**
25.	* **role**	roles	casserole	insole

* Homophones:

sole/soul	What do you call an only spirit or a ghost of a shoe? A sole soul.
pole/poll	What do you call a Polish questionaire? A Pole poll.
role/roll	What do you call a part in a play for a Danish pastry? A roll role.
whole/hole	What do you call the entire empty space a digger makes? The whole hole.
wholly/holy	What do you call something completely sacred? Wholly holy.
style/stile	What do you call the latest fashion in special gates? Stile style.

** Heteronyms:

console ("KAH'n soh'l")/console ("kun SOH'l")

See the complete -ile family on p. 330 in *The Patterns of English Spelling* (TPES); the -ole, p. 331.

Sequential Spelling Level 3 - Teacher's Guide

	61st day	62nd day	63rd day	64th day
1.	* **mind**	minds	minded	minding
2.	* **remind**	**reminds**	reminded	reminding
3.	reminder	reminders	mastermind	masterminded
4.	bind	binds	bound	binding
5.	grind	grinds	ground	grinding
6.	**blind**	**blinds**	blinded	blinding
7.	**kind**	**kinds**	kinder	kindest
8.	** **wind**	** **winds**	** **wound**	winding
9.	rewind	rewinds	rewound	rewinding
10.	**mankind**	hind	hindsight	hindquarter
11.	mind-set	mindful	simple-minded	open-minded
12.	narrow-minded	feeble-minded	absent-minded	evil-minded
13.	** **wind**	** **winds**	windy	windiest
14.	rescind	rescinds	rescinded	rescinding
15.	cinder	cinders	crosswind	headwind
16.	whirlwind	woodwind	tailwind	downwind
17.	upwind	headwind	windmill	windfall
18.	**window**	windshield	windbag	windbreak
19.	**It's too bad.**	**It's too hot.**	**although**	**though**
20.	**boo**	* **boos**	booed	booing
21.	taboo	taboos	bamboo	peek-a-boo
22.	tattoo	tattoos	tattooed	tattooing
23.	shampoo	shampoos	shampooed	shampooing
24.	woo	woos	wooed	wooing
25.	* **shoo**	* **shoos**	* **shooed**	* **shooing**

* **Homophones**:

mined/mind   What do you call an intellect that has been tapped? A mined mind.

shoo/shoe   What do you call footgear that is thrown at a cat? A shoo shoe.

** **Heteronyms**:

wind ("WIN'd")/wind ("WYH'n-d")   It's hard for a pitcher to wind up with the wind in his face.

wound ("WOW'n-d")/wound ("WOO'n-d")   He wound up his watch. His war wound hurt.

See the complete – ind family on p. 229 in *The Patterns of English Spelling* (TPES); the -oo family p. 312.

	65th day	66th day	67th day	68th day
1.	**canoe**	canoes	canoed	canoeing
2.	* **shoe**	shoes	shoed	shoeing
3.	horseshoe	horseshoes	soft-shoe	snowshoes
4.	shoebox	shoeshine	shoetree	shoelaces
5.	**moon**	moons	honeymoon	honeymoons
6.	**spoon**	spoons	spooned	spooning
7.	**balloon**	balloons	ballooned	ballooning
8.	harpoon	harpoons	harpooned	harpooning
9.	lampoon	lampoons	baboon	baboons
10.	platoon	platoons	cartooned	cartooning
11.	maroon	maroons	marooned	raccoon
12.	**cartoon**	cartoons	cartoonist	cartoonists
13.	swoon	swoons	swooned	swooning
14.	saloon	saloons	teaspoon	tablespoon
15.	buffoon	monsoon	pontoon	spittoon
16.	cocoon	typhoon	tycoon	**loon**
17.	moonlight	moonlighting	forenoon	afternoon
18.	**boot**	boots	booted	booting
19.	**shoot**	shoots	shot	shooting
20.	shooter	* **booty**	coot	cootie
21.	hoot	* **bootie**	booties	cooties
22.	** **root**	roots	rooted	rooting
23.	scoot	scoots	scooted	scooter
24.	troubleshoot	troubleshooting	troubleshooter	outshoot
25.	galoot	in cahoots	shootout	a moot point

* Homophones:

shoe/shoo   What do you call footgear thrown at an animal? A shoo shoe.

booty/bootie   What do you call a bonanza of baby shoes? Bootie booty.

** Heteronyms

root "ROO't"/ root "RuuT" In some dialects, the word root rhymes with boot and in others in rhymes with foot.

See the complete -oe family on p. 313 in *The Patterns of English Spelling* (TPES); the -oon, p. 422; the -oot, p. 429.

	69th day	70th day	71st day	72nd day
1.	**foot**	**feet**	footed	**footing**
2.	pussyfoot	pussyfoots	pussyfooted	pussyfooting
3.	underfoot	surefooted	afoot	surefooted
4.	barefoot	bare feet	barefooted	flatfooted
5.	football	footwork	footfall	footrest
6.	soot	sooty	lead-footed	**though**
7.	chamber	chambers	chambered	**although**
8.	ember	embers	**although**	* **throughout**
9.	December	December's weather	**thoroughly**	* **through**
10.	**member**	members	membership	thoroughness
11.	**remember**	**remembers**	**remembered**	**remembering**
12.	limber	limbers	limbered	limbering
13.	* timber	timbers	timberland	timberline
14.	encumber	encumbers	encumbered	encumbering
15.	cucumber	cucumbers	bomber[1]	bombers
16.	**number**	**numbers**	numbered	numbering
17.	outnumber	outnumbers	outnumbered	outnumbering
18.	beachcomber[1]	beachcombers	climber[1]	climbers
19.	humble	humbles	humbled	humbling
20.	tumble	tumbles	tumbling	tumblers
21.	jumble	stumble	stumbled	stumbling
22.	fumble	fumbles	fumbled	fumbling
23.	mumble	mumbles	mumbled	mumbling
24.	rumble	rumbles	rumbled	rumbling
25.	grumble	grumbles	grumbled	grumbling

* Homophones:

timber/timbre   What do you call a wooden voice? Timber timbre.

throughout/threw out   Throughout the game, the umpire threw out new baseballs.

See the complete -mber family on p. 639 in *The Patterns of English Spelling*; the -umble, p. 606.

[1]*Beachcomber, climber* and *bomber* all have a silent letter b. See p. 958 in *The Patterns of English Spelling* for more examples of this pattern.

	73rd day	74th day	75th day	76th day
1.	fund	funds	funded	funding
2.	refund	refunds	refunded	refunding
3.	**under**	underage	underarm	underdog
4.	thunder	thunders	thundered	thundering
5.	blunder	blunders	blundered	blundering
6.	plunder	plunders	plundering	plundered
7.	**understand**	misunderstand	**misunderstanding**	misunderstood
8.	thunderstorm	thunderhead	thunderbolt	underwent
9.	bundle	bundles	bundled	bundling
10.	trundle	trundles	trundled	trundling
11.	**handle**	handles	handled	**handling**
12.	mishandle	mishandles	mishandled	handlers
13.	candle	candles	dandle	dandling
14.	fondle	fondles	fondled	fondling
15.	dwindle	dwindles	dwindled	dwindling
16.	swindle	swindled	swindling	swindlers
17.	kindle	kindled	kindles	kindling
18.	rekindle	rekindles	rekindled	rekindling
19.	**hunt**	hunts	hunting	hunters
20.	bunt	bunted	bunting	bluntly
21.	blunt	blunts	blunted	runts
22.	grunt	grunts	grunted	grunting
23.	stunt	stunts	manhunt	headhunter
24.	**front**	storefronts	frontage	confrontation
25.	confront	affronted	forefront	confronting

> **NOTE:** In English spelling there is a common reversal in sounds. What should be -del (as it is in the name Handel) is spelled -dle. The ending pattern -le is extremely common as in pickle despite the fact that it really should be -el as in nickel.

See the complete -nder family on p. 642 in *The Patterns of English Spelling* (TPES); the -ndle, p. 607; the -unt, p. 249.

Sequential Spelling Level 3 - Teacher's Guide

	77th day	78th day	79th day	80th day
1.	**ask**	asks	asked	asking
2.	mask	masks	masked	masking
3.	unmask	unmasks	unmasked	unmasking
4.	**task**	tasks	**basket**	baskets
5.	cask	casks	casket	caskets
6.	flask	flasks	gaskets	basketball
7.	* **bask**	* **basks**	basked	basking
8.	**desk**	desks	news desk	pesky
9.	**risk**	risks	risked	**risky**
10.	frisk	frisks	frisked	frisky
11.	whisk	whisks	whisked	* **whisky**
12.	whisker	whiskers	whisking	* **whiskey**
13.	* **disk**	* **disks**	* **disc**	* **discs**
14.	husk	husks	husked	husky
15.	musk	dusk	tusk	tusks
16.	mollusk	* **brusk**	musky	a corn husker
17.	ranch	ranches	rancher	ranchers
18.	branch	branches	branched	branching
19.	blanch	blanches	blanched	blanching
20.	franchise	franchises	**thoroughly**	**although**
21.	launch	launches	launched	launching
22.	paunch	paunches	paunchy	rocket launchers
23.	haunch	haunches	staunch	raunch
24.	**tsk, tsk**[1]	**tsk, tsk**	**psst!**[2]	**psst!**
25.	beauty	beautifully	beautifying	beauties

* **Homophones**:

bask/Basque	To bask in the sun is enjoyable. Do you have a Basque beret?
whisky/whiskey	Some people drink whisky. Others drink whiskey.
disk/disc	Do you have the word disc on your floppy disk?
brusk/brusque	Writers generally prefer the fancy brusque to brusk.

See the complete -sk family on p. 271 in (TPES); the -nch, pp. 206-207.

[1]*Tsk* does not rhyme with *whisk*. *Tsk* is the sound you make to show disapproval by placing your tongue against your front teeth and making a clicking sound. Similarly, *psst* also has no vowel.

[2]*Psst* is the sound you make to get somebody's attention when you don't want others to know you're doing it.

Evaluation Test #2
(After 80 Days)

		Pattern being tested	Lesson word is in
1.	Did your neighbor sell his pr**operty**?	operty	36
2.	The little kids spl**ashed** around in the pool all day.	ashed	39
3.	We were simply cr**ushed** to find we weren't invited.	ushed	39
4.	The thief was caught hiding in the b**ushes**.	ushes	42
5.	You can make paste by mixing fl**our** with water.	our	45
6.	Do the rains in April bring on the fl**owers** in May?	owers	46
7.	Oh, how I hate to get up in the m**orning**.	orning	48
8.	We rep**orted** the accident to the police.	orted	51
9.	Sometimes names are hard to pron**ounce**.	ounce	51
10.	My sister is taking up acc**ounting** in college.	ounting	52
11.	I wish you would stop cl**owning** around.	owning	56
12.	I wonder what the Mona Lisa was sm**iling** about.	iling	56
13.	Would you like a rept**ile** for a pet?	ile	57
14.	We won a cons**olation** prize.	olation	60
15.	I sometimes have to be rem**inded** about the time.	inded	63
16.	Would somebody please open that w**indow** for me?	indow	61
17.	Have you ever fished with a bamb**oo** pole?	oo	63
18.	It's no fun to be mar**ooned** on a desert island.	ooned	67
19.	How would you like to be rem**embered**?	embered	71
20.	I wish they would stop gr**umbling** all the time.	umbling	72

	81st day	82nd day	83rd day	84th day
1.	**bench**	benches	benched	benching
2.	**wrench**	wrenches	wrenched	wrenching
3.	clench	clenches	clenched	clenching
4.	stench	drench	**drenched**	thirst quencher
5.	quench	**quenches**	quenched	quenching
6.	trench	trenches	* **entrenched**	* **entrenching**
7.	* entrench	stench	* **intrenched**	* **intrenching**
8.	**inch**	inches	inched	inching
9.	**pinch**	pinches	pinched	pinching
10.	* **lynch**	lynches	lynched	lynching
11.	clinch	clinches	clinched	clinching
12.	finch	finches	pinchers	clinchers
13.	flinch	flinches	flinched	flinching
14.	cinch	cinches	cinched	cinching
15.	winch	winches	winched	winching
16.	The Grinch	The Grinch's heart	Wednesday	Wednesday
17.	**bunch**	bunches	bunched	bunching
18.	**hunch**	hunches	hunched	hunching
19.	**punch**	punches	punched	punching
20.	**crunch**	crunches	crunched	crunching
21.	brunch	brunches	luncheon	luncheons
22.	**lunch**	lunches	lunched	lunching
23.	munch	munches	munched	munchies
24.	scrunch	scrunches	scrunched up	honeybunch
25.	* **throughout**	**thoroughly**	**although**	**though**

* Homophones:

entrench/intrench   Most writers prefer entrench to intrench.

See the complete -nch families on pp. 206-207 in *The Patterns of English Spelling*.

	85th day	86th day	87th day	88th day
1.	**church**	churches	The church's pastor	**honest**
2.	lurch	lurches	lurched	lurching
3.	**perch**	perches	perched	perching
4.	**attach**	attaches	attached	attaching
5.	detach	detaches	detached	detaching
6.	reattach	reattaches	reattached	reattaching
7.	attachment	attachments	detachment	detachments
8.	**match**	matches	matched	matching
9.	patch	patches	patched	patching
10.	dispatch	dispatches	dispatched	dispatchers
11.	hatch	hatches	hatched	hatchery
12.	latch	latches	latched	latching
13.	snatch	snatches	snatched	hatcheries
14.	batch	batches	thatched	Catch-22
15.	* **catch**	catches	catching	catchers
16.	**scratch**	**scratches**	scratching	Mrs. Thatcher
17.	unlatch	unlatches	unlatched	unlatching
18.	etch	etches	etched	etching
19.	* **retch**	retches	retched	retching
20.	stretch	stretches	stretched	stretchers
21.	* **wretch**	wretches	*** **wretched**	* farfetched
22.	fetch	fetches	* **far-fetched**	fetching
23.	* **ketch**	ketches	Wednesday's child	most Wednesdays
24.	sketch	sketches	sketched	sketching
25.	Fletch	Fletcher	Fletch's sketches	**honesty**

* **Homophones**:

catch/ketch	A ketch can't catch up to a speedboat.
retch/wretch	What do you call a poor urchin's vomit? Wretch retch.
far-fetched/farfetched	You have your choice. Both are correct.

*** Pronounce the adjective *wretched* ("RET chid"). The verbs ending -etched are pronounced "ETCH't."

See the complete -urch family on p. 520 in *The Patterns of English Spelling* (TPES); the -etch, p. 202; the -ach & -atch, p. 201.

	89th day	90th day	91st day	92nd day
1.	**itch**	**itches**	itched	itching
2.	* **witch**	**witches**	a **witch's** brew	two witches' brooms
3.	switch	switches	switched	switching
4.	**pitch**	pitched	pitching	* **pitchers**
5.	ditch	ditches	ditched	ditching
6.	snitch	snitches	snitching	a last-ditch effort
7.	hitch	hitches	hitched	hitching
8.	twitch	twitches	twitched	twitching
9.	bewitch	bewitches	bewitched	bewitching
10.	**kitchen**	kitchens	* **which**	sandwiches
11.	**picture**	**pictures**	pictured	picturing
12.	lecture	lectures	lectured	lecturing
13.	fracture	fractures	fractured	fracturing
14.	manufacture	manufactures	manufactured	manufacturing
15.	* **maid**	maids	maiden	maidens
16.	raid	raids	raided	raiders
17.	* **braid**	braids	braided	braiding
18.	**afraid**	unpaid	repaid	unrepaid
19.	**laid**	mislaid	bridesmaid	handmaid
20.	mermaid	Medicaid	milkmaid	inlaid
21.	**aid**	aids	aided	aiding
22.	**broad**	broader	broadest	broadly
23.	broadcast	abroad	broadcaster	broadcasting
24.	broadside	broad jump	broad brim	Broadway
25.	broadcloth	**honest**	**honestly**	**honesty**

* **Homophones:**

maid/made	The maid made up a story.
which/witch	Which witch owns the black cat?
pitcher/picture	What do you call a Nolan Ryan photo? A pitcher picture.
braid/brayed	That girl loves to braid her hair. The donkey brayed.

See the complete -itch family on p. 203 in *The Patterns of English Spelling* (TPES); the -cture, p. 923; the -aid, p. 401; the -broad, p. 401.

33

	93rd day	94th day	95th day	96th day
1.	**key**	keys	keyed up	keying
2.	monkey	monkeys	monkeyed	monkeying
3.	**money**	**honey**	turkey	turkeys
4.	volley	volleys	volleyed	volleying
5.	valley	valleys	alley	alleys
6.	jockey	jockeys	abbey	attorney
7.	journey	journeys	journeyed	journeying
8.	pulley	chimney	chop suey	flunkey
9.	curtsey	donkey	galley	kidney
10.	New Jersey	parsley	parslied	chimney
11.	trolley	phooey	baloney	honey
12.	**they**	*** they're**	**they've**	**they'd**
13.	*** grey**[1]	*** greys**[1]	*** greyed**	greying
14.	*** prey**	*** preys**	*** preyed**	praying
15.	**obey**	obeys	obeyed	obeying
16.	disobey	disobeys	disobeyed	disobeying
17.	obedient	obediently	obedience	obedience
18.	disobedient	disobediently	disobedience	disobedience
19.	survey	surveys	surveyed	surveying
20.	convey	conveys	conveyed	conveying
21.	*** hey**	whey	*** trey**	Monterey
22.	**each**	tongue	**tongue**	**tongues**
23.	beach	beaches	beached	beaching
24.	*** leach**	leaches	leached	leaching
25.	bleach	bleaches	bleached	bleachers

* Homophones:

grey/gray	The Britisher wore grey. The American wore gray.
greys/grays/graze	What do you call it when black and white sheep eat together? Greys graze.
greyed/grayed/grade	What do you call a dingy class? A greyed grade or a grayed grade.
prey/pray	Lions prey. We pray.
preys/prays/praise	The lion preys on antelope. A religious person prays, "Praise be to God."
leach/leech	If you could leach a leech, would you?
hey/hay	What do you say to get fodder's attention? Hey, Hay.
trey/tray	A basketball player shoots a trey. A waiter carries a tray.

See the complete -ey family on pp. 306 & 302 in TPES; the -each, p. 437.

[1]Because we read writers who use American spellings and writers who use British spellings, both are given. Teach either or both, whichever you feel is most appropriate for your students.

Sequential Spelling Level 3 - Teacher's Guide

	97th day	98th day	99th day	100th day
1.	**reach**	reaches	**reached**	reaching
2.	**teach**	teaches	**teachers**	**teaching**
3.	**preach**	preaches	preachers	**preaching**
4.	overreach	overreaches	overreached	overreaching
5.	peach	**peaches**	* **beach**	beaches
6.	impeach	impeaches	impeached	impeachment
7.	* **breach**	breaches	breached	breaching
8.	**speech**	speeches	* **beech**	beeches
9.	** (*) **breech**	**breeches**[1]	breeched	breeching
10.	beseech	beseeches	beseeched	beseeching
11.	screech	screeches	screeched	screeching
12.	**able**	**unable**	**ability**	inability
13.	**enable**	enables	**enabled**	enabling
14.	**disable**	**disabled**	**disability**	**abilities**
15.	**table**	tables	tabled	tabling
16.	timetable	timetables	times table	times tables
17.	turntable	turntables	sable	Ken Stabler
18.	**stable**	stables	unstable	**stability**
19.	**cable**	cables	cabled	cabling
20.	fable	fables	fabled	instability
21.	**Bible**	Bibles	**noble**	nobles
22.	ruble	rubles	ennobled	nobility
23.	bauble	bauble	foible	foibles
24.	**double**	doubles	doubled	doubling
25.	**trouble**	**troubles**	**troubled**	**troubling**

* **Homophones**:

beach/beech   It is possible to see a beech tree while you're at the beach.

breach/breech   You shouldn't breach a contract. A breech birth is dangerous.

* **Heteronyms**:

breech ("breech")/breech ("brich")   The preferred pronunciation is "breech," but the correct pronunciation of breeches   is always "brich iz" as in "He's too big for his breeches."

See the complete -each family on p. 437 in (TPES); the -eech, p. 437; -ble, p, 610.

[1]The word breeches rhymes with ditches and witches!

	101st day	102nd day	103rd day	104th day
1.	**star**	stars	**starred**	**starring**
2.	**scar**	**scars**	**scarred**	**scarring**
3.	spar	spars	**sparred**	**sparring**
4.	disbar	disbars	disbarred	disbarring
5.	par	pars	**parred**	**parring**
6.	char	charcoal	* charred	charring
7.	cigar	cigars	seminar	streetcar
8.	sandbar	superstar	* **czar**	**czars**
9.	bazaar	Zanzibar	* **tsar**	**tsars**
10.	**war**	wars	* **warred**	warring
11.	* **ward**	wards	warded	warding
12.	**warm**	warms	warmed	warming
13.	swarm	swarms	swarmed	swarming
14.	* **warn**	warns	warned	warning
15.	warp	warps	warped	warping
16.	wart	warts	prewar	postwar
17.	**quart**	* **quarts**	* **quartz**	warden
18.	award	awards	awarded	awarding
19.	**reward**	rewards	rewarded	rewarding
20.	warrant	warrants	warranted	warrantee
21.	dwarf	dwarfs	dwarves	dwarfing
22.	wharf	wharfs	wharves	warriors
23.	**quarter**	quarters	quartered	quartering
24.	quarterly	quarterlies	quarrelsome	warmest
25.	forewarn	forewarns	forewarned	forewarning

* Homophones:

charred/chard	What do you call burnt greens? Charred chard.
czar/tsar	Americans generally prefer czar; the British, tsar.
quarts/quartz	Why don't they measure quartz by quarts?
warn/worn	Did you warn them that the clothes they are buying have been worn before?

To the Teacher: The letter U in qUart, qUartz, qUarter, qUarrel, & qUarry is really the consonant W (DOUBLE U") – not a vowel. The letter Q in QU words sounds as a K; i.e, QU=KW. The W- control operates in the word "WHARF" because the sound /W/ actually follows the /H/ sound. This is true in all the WH- words in which the W is pronounced. That is, the WH- words are normally pronounced /HW/ or just /W/. This "REVERSAL" of sounds (or dropping of the /H/ sound) is rather easy to teach children to read and spell.

See the complete -ar family on p. 501 (TPES); the -war-, p. 502.

Sequential Spelling Level 3 - Teacher's Guide

	105th day	106th day	107th day	108th day
1.	**quarrel**	quarrels	(Am.) quarreled	(Am.) quarreling
2.	quarrelsome	it's too much	(Br.) quarrelled	(Br.) quarrelling
3.	quarry	quarries	quarried	quarrying
4.	Scotch	Scotches	hopscotch	topnotch
5.	botch	botches	botched	botching
6.	notch	notches	notched	notching
7.	blotch	blotches	crotch	crotches
8.	Dutch	Dutchman	Dutchmen	it's too bad
9.	clutch	clutches	clutched	clutching
10.	hutch	hutches	Hutch	Hutchinson
11.	crutch	crutches	**cousin**	**two cousins**
12.	**such**	**too much**	much too much	lost its collar
13.	**touch**	**touches**	touched	touching
14.	retouch	retouches	retouched	retouching
15.	untouchable	touchdown	touchy	quality
16.	Butch	Butch's car	butchery	equality
17.	butcher	butchers	butchered	butchering
18.	**watch**	**watches**	**watched**	**watching**
19.	swatch	swatches	watchman	watchmen
20.	watchdog	watcheye	watchful	watchfulness
21.	watchtower	watchword	stopwatch	watchmaker
22.	swat	swats	swatted	swatting
23.	squat	squats	squatted	squatters
24.	kumquat	kumquats	**suave**[1]	watertight
25.	**fly swatter**	swatters	Waterloo	watermark

> **To the Teacher:** The letter U in qUart, qUartz, qUarter, qUarrel, qUarry and sUave is really the consonant W (DOUBLE U") · not a vowel. The letter Q in QU words sounds as a K; i.e., QU=KW. The W- CONTROL operates in the word "WHARF" because the sound /W/ actually follows the /H/ sound as is true in all the WH- words in which the W is sounded. That is, the WH- words are normally pronounced /HW/ or just /W/. This very regular "REVERSAL" of sounds (or dropping of the /H/ sound) is rather easy to teach children to read and spell.

See the complete -otch family on p. 204 in *The Patterns of English Spelling* (TPES); the -utch, p. 205; the –atch, p. 201.

[1]See the wa- controlled words on p. 504 of *The Patterns of English Spelling*.

	109th day	110th day	111th day	112th day
1.	* **road**	roads	carloads	truckloads
2.	**load**	loads	loaded	loading
3.	reload	unloaded	overloaded	toll road
4.	railroad	crossroad	off-road	payload
5.	goad	goads	goaded	goading
6.	**leap**	leaps	leaping	leaper
7.	* **cheap**	cheaper	cheapest	cheaply
8.	reap	reaps	reaping	grim reaper
9.	heap	heaps	heaped	heaping
10.	* **Greece**	Greek	Greeks	Greece
11.	fleece	fleeces	fleeced	fleecing
12.	**speed**	speeds	speeding	speeders
13.	**feed**	**feeding**	**fed**	feeders
14.	**bleed**	**bleeding**	**bled**	bleeders
15.	* **need**	needs	needle	needled
16.	**weeds**	weedy	weeder	weeding
17.	* **seed**	* **seeder**	seedy	seeded
18.	deed	deeded	thimbleweed	milkweed
19.	breed	breeding	* **bred**	stockbreeding
20.	* **heed**	heeded	indeed	nosebleed
21.	exceed	exceeded	exceedingly	exceeds
22.	proceed	proceeds	proceedings	procedures
23.	**succeed**	succeeds	succeeded	**success**
24.	**seemed**	seemingly	self-esteem	* teeming
25.	deem	redeem	redeeming	redeemer

* Homophones:

road/rowed/ rode	We rowed across a river and rode in a taxi on a bumpy road.
cheap/cheep	What do you call an inexpensive chirp? A cheap cheep.
Greece/grease	What does a Greek call olive oil? Greece grease.
seed/cede	What do you call to surrender a potential plant? To cede a seed.
seeder/cedar	What do you call a wooden planter? A cedar seeder.
he'd/heed	What do you call it if a man would pay attention? He'd heed.
teem/team	When rivers teem with fish, there is a team of fishermen.
bred/bread	This wheat was especially bred to be made into bread.

See the complete -oad family on p. 403 in *The Patterns of English Spelling* (TPES), -eap p. 424, -eece, p. 432, -eed p. 402, -eem, 418.

	113th day	114th day	115th day	116th day
1.	**sheet**	**sheets**	sheeting	sweetness
2.	* **meet**	**meets**	**met**	**meetings**
3.	greet	greeted	greetings	sweeteners
4.	tweet	tweets	tweeted	tweeter
5.	**sweet**	sweets	sweeten	sweetened
6.	* **feet**	skeet	* **beets**	* **parakeets**
7.	fleet	sleet	discreet	discretion
8.	sweetheart	sweet-talk	indiscreet	indiscretion
9.	* **high**	* **higher**	highest	highway
10.	**sigh**	* **sighs**	* **sighed**	sighing
11.	high school	sky-high	knee-high	nigh
12.	thigh	Captain Bligh	thighbone	heigh-ho
13.	* **right**	rights	righted	* **righting**
14.	**fight**	fighter	fighting	fighters
15.	* **sight**	sights	sighted	unsightly
16.	**light**	lights	lighted	lighting
17.	lighter	lightest	lightly	thunder and **lightning**
18.	lighten	lightens	lightened	**lightening**
19.	delight	delights	delightful	delightfully
20.	* **night**	days and nights	tightfisted	headlights
21.	* **knight**	knights	knighted	knighthood
22.	swordfight	candlelight	dogfight	bullfights
23.	**flight**	flights	flighted	millwright
24.	**frighten**	frightens	**frightened**	frightening
25.	**tighten**	tightens	**tightened**	tightening

* **Homophones**:

meet/meat/mete	Mr. E meet Mrs. E. We eat meat. Judges mete out punishment.
feet/feat	What do you call a great jump? A feet feat.
high/hi/hie	Hi there! Hie yourself there. High up in the sky.
higher/hire	What is higher than a kite? Would you hire someone who was?
sighed/side	He sighed, "Whose side are you on?"
sighs/size	She sighs about her size.
night/knight	What do you call a Mr. by day and Sir after six? A night knight.
sight/site/cite	A judge can cite a site for being a sight.
right/rite/write/wright	Can a Wright write a rite right?

See the complete -eet family on p. 427 in *The Patterns of English Spelling* (TPES); the -igh, p. 308; the -ight, p. 428.

	117th day	118th day	119th day	120th day
1.	**ought**	ought to	ought not to	ought to
2.	**fought**	fought	That's too bad.	forethought
3.	**bought**	bought	thoughtful	afterthought
4.	**brought**	thoughtful	thoughtfully	thoughtfulness
5.	**thought**	**thoughts**	**laugh**	laughs
6.	wrought	overwrought	laughter	laughter
7.	* **taught**	self-taught	caught	**ghost**
8.	distraught	onslaught	**honest**	**honesty**
9.	slaughter	slaughters	slaughtered	slaughtering
10.	**daughter**	daughters	my daughter's friends	Cosby's daughters' friends
11.	for naught	naughty	naughtier	naughtiest
12.	dreadnaught	**thoroughly**	**although**	* **throughout**
13.	* **taut**	astronaut	juggernaut	**although**
14.	**end**	ends	ended	ending
15.	**friend**	friends	**friendly**	friendship
16.	**bend**	**bends**	**bent/bended**	bending
17.	**lend**	* **lends**	**lent**	lending
18.	**send**	sends	*sent	sending
19.	**spend**	spends	**spent**	spending
20.	fend	fends	fending	fenders
21.	defend	defended	defenders	defensive
22.	offend	offended	offenders	offensive
23.	ascend	ascended	* **ascent**	ascension
24.	descend	descended	descent	descendant
25.	condescend	condescended	condescending	condescension

* **Homophones:**

taught/taut	We were taught that a tight rope is taut.
sent/cent	We sent you a cent.
ascent/a scent/a cent	What do you call cheap perfume going up? A cent a scent ascent.
lends/lens	What an eye doctor does when he rents free half a pair of glasses. Lends lens.

See the complete -aught family on p. 430 and the -end on p. 208 in *The Patterns of English Spelling*.

Sequential Spelling Level 3 - Teacher's Guide

Evaluation Test #3
(After 120 Days)

		Pattern being tested	Lesson word is in
1.	I hope our neighbors weren't sw**indled.**	indled	74
2.	We **asked** them to come to our house first.	asked	79
3.	They sent us several b**askets** of flowers.	askets	80
4.	They had to trim several br**anches** off the tree.	anches	78
5.	Water really qu**enches** your thirst.	enches	82
6.	Children should be taught to never play with m**atches.**	atches	86
7.	The injured player was carried out on a str**etcher.**	etcher	88
8.	If there's anything I hate, it's listening to l**ectures.**	ectures	90
9.	The player suffered a fr**acture.**	acture	89
10.	It's hard to p**icture** a president in hair curlers.	icture	89
11.	It's fun to play v**olley**ball.	olley	93
12.	You shouldn't have disob**eyed** orders.	eyed	95
13.	We watched the ball game from the bl**eachers.**	eachers	96
14.	It's time we called a scr**eeching** halt to this nonsense.	eeching	100
15.	Nitroglycerin is highly unst**able.**	able	99
16.	Everybody has all kinds of different **abilities**.	abilities	100
17.	Do you remember who st**arred** in Gone With the Wind?	arred	103
18.	How many times do you have to be w**arned** about that?	arned	103
19.	When I hurt my foot, I had to walk on cr**utches.**	utches	106
20.	I love to hear the piano played with a light t**ouch.**	ouch	105

41

	121st day	122nd day	123rd day	124th day
1.	befriend	befriends	befriended	befriending
2.	**blend**	blends	blending	blenders
3.	mend	* **mends**	mended	mending
4.	commend	commends	commended	commending
5.	recommend	recommended	recommending	recommendation
6.	amend	amends	amended	amendment
7.	comprehend	comprehended	comprehensive	comprehension
8.	apprehend	apprehending	apprehensive	apprehension
9.	pend	* **pends**	pended	Peter Pender
10.	**depend**	* **depends**	dependent	dependence
11.	suspend	suspends	suspending	suspension
12.	expend	expended	expending	expensive
13.	append	appended	appendix	appendage
14.	wend	wended	Wendy went Wednesday.	independence
15.	tend	* **tends**	tended	tending
16.	**attend**	attended	**two * attendants**	attention
17.	pretend	pretended	pretending	pretension
18.	**intend**	intended	intensive	intention
19.	contend	contended	contenders	contention
20.	extend	extended	extensive	extension
21.	overextend	overextending	overextended	overextension
22.	distend	distends	distended	distending
23.	portend	portends	portending	portent
24.	vend	vends	vending	vendors
25.	trends	dividends	legends	reverends

* **Homophones**:

mends/men's	A seamstress often mends men's clothing.
pends/pens	Who pends when a patent on pens is pending?
tends/tens	A pair of tens tends to beat most pairs.
attendants/attendance	What do you call the roll call record of helpers. Attendants' attendance.

See the complete -end family on p. 228 in *The Patterns of English Spelling* (TPES).

	125th day	126th day	127st day	128th day
1.	**any**	**anyone**	**anybody**	**anywhere**
2.	**anything**	**any place**	**many**	**although**
3.	rainy	rainier	rainiest	We're all **through**.
4.	brainy	brainier	brainiest	We're **thorough**.
5.	**tiny**	tinier	tiniest	**thoroughly**
6.	**shiny**	shinier	shiniest	**thought**
7.	whiny	whinier	whiniest	thoughtful
8.	pony	ponies	a pony's tail	the ponies' riders
9.	bony	agony	agonies	agonize
10.	stony	stonier	stoniest	thoughtfully
11.	**crony**	cronies	It's too bad	thoroughness
12.	ceremony	ceremonies	ceremonial	thoughtfulness
13.	matrimony	matrimonial	maternity	matriarchy
14.	patrimony	patrimonial	paternity	patriarchy
15.	frater	fraternal	fraternity	fraternities
16.	loony	loonies	sorority	sororities
17.	testimony	testimonial	testament	testify
18.	**puny**	punier	puniest	Tiffany
19.	corny	cornier	corniest	Germany
20.	brawny	brawnier	brawniest	monotony
21.	mahogany	accompany	Albany	botany
22.	monotony	destiny	destination	larceny
23.	mutiny	peony	peonies	gluttony
24.	scrutiny	felony	felonies	ebony
25.	balcony	balconies	colony	colonies

See the complete -ny families on pp. 717 and 718 in *The Patterns of English Spelling*.

43

	129th day	130th day	131st day	132nd day
1.	goof	goofed	goofy	goofiest
2.	**roof**	roofs	roofer	roofing
3.	**proof**	proofs	bulletproof	soundproof
4.	**prove**	proves	proved	**proving**
5.	hoof	hoofs	hooves	tamperproof
6.	goofproof	foolproof	waterproof	waterproofing
7.	spoof	spoofs	spoofed	spoofing
8.	* **half**	halves	halved	halving
9.	**one-half**	two loaves	sugarloaf	**laughter**
10.	**loaf**	loafs	loafed	loafing
11.	**laugh**	laughs	laughed	laughing
12.	spook	spooks	spooked	spooking
13.	kook	kooks	gadzooks	spooky
14.	**folk**	folks	* **yolk**	yolks
15.	**took**	shook	It's too hot.	It's too big.
16.	**look**	looks	looked	looking
17.	**cook**	cooks	cooked	**cookie**
18.	**book**	books	pocketbook	guidebook
19.	rook	rooks	rookie	rookies
20.	crook	crooks	crooked	cookbook
21.	brook	brooks	hook	hooked
22.	overlook	overlooked	unlooked for	partook
23.	donnybrook	jokebook	notebooks	matchbooks
24.	workbooks	scrapbook	yearbooks	passbook
25.	bookkeeper	bookkeeping	bookshelf	bookshelves

* **Homophones**:

yolk/yoke   What would you call an ox collar made with no egg whites? A yolk yoke.

have to/half to   To split evenly means you have to give half to the other person.

See the complete -ook family on pages 409 in *The Patterns of English Spelling*; the -olk, p. 409; the -oof, p. 407; the -ove, p. 326; the -oaf, p. 407.

Sequential Spelling Level 3 - Teacher's Guide

	133rd day	134th day	135th day	136th day
1.	* **oar**	oars	oarlock	oarsmen
2.	* **soar**	soars	soared	soaring
3.	roar	roars	roared	roaring
4.	uproar	uproarious	**although**	**thoroughly**
5.	* **boar**	* **boars**	* **throughout**	thoroughness
6.	* **liar**	liars	pliers	**though**
7.	**sorry**	lorry	lorries	hurriedly
8.	**worry**	worries	worried	worrying
9.	**hurry**	hurries	hurried	hurrying
10.	scurry	scurries	scurried	scurrying
11.	flurry	flurries	It's too good.	It hurt its wing.
12.	**carry**	**carries**	**carried**	**carrying**
13.	* **marry**	**marries**	**married**	**marrying**
14.	* **ferry**	ferries	ferried	ferrying
15.	* **merry**	merrily	merriment	merry-go-round
16.	* **berry**	berries	loganberries	mulberry
17.	cackleberry[1]	cranberries	huckleberry	strawberries
18.	blackberry	blueberries	thimbleberry	raspberries
19.	* **fur**	furs	furrier	**honesty**
20.	purr	purrs	purred	purring
21.	spur	spurs	spurred	spurring
22.	burr	burrs	Aaron Burr	occurrence
23.	slur	slurs	slurred	slurring
24.	**occur**	occurs	**occurred**	occurring
25.	recur	recurs	recurred	recurring

* **Homophones**:

oar/or/ore   What do you call a choice between a paddle and metallic earth? Oar or ore.

soar/sore   To fly high is to soar. To have aches and pains is to be sore.

boar/bore   What do you call a unexciting male pig? A boar bore.

liar/lyre   What do you call a dishonest harp? A lyre liar.

fairy/ferry   What do you call a boat for magical people? A fairy ferry.

marry/merry   We make merry when we marry.

berry/bury   Will you bury the berry?

fir/fur   What do you call hair on an evergreen? Fir fur.

See the complete -oar family on p. 532; -rry family on p. 706; ur family, p. 520 in *The Patterns of English Spelling.*

[1]Cackleberries are eggs in several dialects.

	137th day	138th day	139th day	140th day
1.	reoccur	reoccurs	reoccurred	reoccurring
2.	blur	blurs	blurred	blurring
3.	concur	concurs	concurred	concurrent
4.	murmur	murmurs	murmured	murmuring
5.	verb	verbs	verbal	verbally
6.	** **herb**	herbs	herbal	proverbs
7.	adverb	adverbs	proverb	proverbial
8.	superb	It's too big.	It's to go.	found its way
9.	* **forward**	forwards	forwarded	forwarding
10.	hazard	hazards	hazarded	hazardous
11.	**standard**	standards	nonstandard	custard
12.	* **mustard**	haggard	laggard	sluggard
13.	orchard	orchards	billiards	innards
14.	Spaniard	Spaniards	** **leeward**	dullard
15.	windward	southward	downward	straightforward
16.	lizard	lizards	blizzard	Packard
17.	leopard	leopards	backward	homeward
18.	awkward	coward	cowards	cowardly
19.	steward	afterwards	wizard	**vineyard**
20.	**beard**	beards	bearded	bearding
21.	Bluebeard	Blackbeard	hummingbird	mockingbird
22.	* **heard**	overheard	unheard of	23rd
23.	**bird**	birds	third	twenty-third
24.	songbird	lovebird	early bird	thirty-third
25.	blackbird	redbird	whirlybird	thirds

* Homophones:

forward/foreword	What do you call a brazen introduction? A forward foreword.
mustard/mustered	Pass the mustard, please. He was mustered out of the army.
heard/herd	Did that group of cows hear you? Yes, the herd heard me.
leeward/lured	To be lured leeward is to be coaxed to the non-windward side.

** Heteronyms:

herb ("HUR'b")/herb ("UR'b")	The British pronounce the H in herb. Americans don't.
leeward ("LOO'r-d")/leeward ("LEE wurd")	The nautical usage is "LOO'r-d"; landlubbers say "LEE wurd."

See the complete -ur family on p. 520 in *The Patterns of English Spelling*; wor-, p. 503; -erb, p. 511; -ard, p. 506; -eard, p. 533; -ird, p. 514.

Sequential Spelling Level 3 - Teacher's Guide

	141st day	142nd day	143rd day	144th day
1.	curd	curds and whey	absurd	absurdly
2.	curdle	curdles	curdled	curdling
3.	hurdle	hurdles	hurdled	hurdling
4.	hurdler	hurdlers	absurdity	absurdities
5.	Earl	Earl's stories	earl	earlier
6.	Pearl	Pearl's songs	**early**	earliest
7.	**girl**	girls	a **girl's** dress	**girls**' dresses
8.	swirl	swirls	swirled	swirling
9.	twirl	twirls	twirled	twirling
10.	whirl	whirls	whirled	whirling
11.	whirlpool	whirlwind	Shirley	Shirley's girls
12.	**firm**	firms	firmed	firming
13.	affirm	affirms	affirmed	affirmative
14.	confirm	confirms	confirmed	confirmation
15.	squirm	squirms	squirmed	squirming
16.	form	forms	formed	forming
17.	format	formative	formation	formations
18.	**inform**	informs	informed	**information**
19.	misinform	misinforms	misinformed	misinformation
20.	uniform	uniforms	uniformity	informative
21.	transform	transforms	transformed	transformation
22.	**perform**	performs	performed	performance
23.	conform	conforms	conformed	conformity
24.	deform	deforms	deformed	deformity
25.	norm	norms	normal	normality

See the complete -ord family on page 516 in *The Patterns of English Spelling*; -urd, p. 520; -irl, p. 514; -earl, p. 533; -irm, p. 515; -orm, p. 517.

	145th day	146th day	147th day	148th day
1.	**barn**	barns	barnyard	barnyards
2.	darn	darns	darned	darning needle
3.	**yarn**	yarns	Mr. Garner	Mrs. Garner's husband
4.	varnish	varnishes	varnished	varnishing
5.	tarnish	tarnishes	tarnished	tarnishing
6.	harness	harnesses	harnessed	harnessing
7.	* **earn**	earns	earned	**earning**
8.	**learn**	learns	learned	**learning**
9.	yearn	yearns	yearned	yearning
10.	learner	learners	earnest	earnestly
11.	**burn**	burns	burned	burning
12.	**turn**	turns	turned	turning
13.	**return**	returns	returned	returning
14.	* **urn**	urns	burner	burners
15.	spurn	spurns	spurned	spurning
16.	churn	churns	churned	churning
17.	sunburn	sunburns	sunburned	sunburning
18.	windburn	windburns	windburned	windburning
19.	turnip	turnips	harpy	harpies
20.	harp	harps	harped	harping
21.	carp	carps	carped	carping
22.	carpet	carpets	carpeted	carpeting
23.	tarp	tarps	sharpener	sharpeners
24.	**sharp**	sharps	sharpie	sharpies
25.	**sharpen**	sharpens	sharpened	sharpening

* **Homophones**:

earn/urn   What is another way of saying "to deserve a vase"? To earn an urn.

See the complete --earn family on page 533 in *The Patterns of English Spelling*; -urn, p. 521; -arp, p. 502.

	149th day	150th day	151st day	152nd day
1.	warp	warps	warped	warping
2.	chirp	chirps	chirped	chirping
3.	twerp	twerps	purple	purple
4.	**first**	twenty-first	thirty-first	forty-first
5.	1st	21st	31st	41st
6.	first-born	first-class	first-hand	We're not **through**
7.	**thirst**	thirsts	thirsted	thirsting
8.	thirsty	thirstier	thirstiest	Martian
9.	harsh	harshly	harshness	martial law
10.	marsh	marshes	marshmallow	marshmallows
11.	* **marshal**	marshals	marshaled	marshaling
12.	Mr. * **Marshall**	Miss Marshall	marshalled	marshalling
13.	**boss**	bosses	bossed	bossing
14.	bossy	bossier	bossiest	mossy
15.	**loss**	losses	moss	mosses
16.	Ross	Ross's losses	across	glossy
17.	**cross**	crosses	crossed	crossings
18.	doublecross	doublecrosses	doublecrossed	doublecrossing
19.	gloss	glosses	glossed	glossing
20.	gross	grosses	grossed	grossing
21.	engross	engrosses	engrossed	engrossing
22.	grossly	* **grosser**	grossest	**grocery**
23.	* **grocer**	* **grocer**	grocers	**groceries**
24.	**forest**	forests	forester	forestry
25.	**interest**	**interests**	**interested**	**interesting**

* Homophones:

marshal/Marshall/martial   What do you call a militant lawman?   A martial marshal.

grosser/grocer   What do you call a more vulgar food seller?   A grosser grocer.

See the complete -arp family on page 508 in *The Patterns of English Spelling*; war-, p. 502; -irp, p. 515; -irst, p. 515; -arsh, p. 509; -oss, p. 159; -est, p. 234.

	153rd day	154th day	155th day	156th day
1.	**coast**	coasts	coasted	coasting
2.	boast	boasts	boasted	boasting
3.	**roast**	roasts	roasted	roasting
4.	**toast**	toasts	toasted	toasting
5.	toaster	toasters	coaster	coasters
6.	boastful	boastfully	roaster	roasters
7.	**pity**	pities	pitied	pitying
8.	**city**	**cities**	**pitiful**	pitifully
9.	**beauty**	beauties	**beautiful**	beautifully
10.	**duty**	**duties**	dutiful	dutifully
11.	**blue**	blues	bluing	Tuesday
12.	trueblue	**Tuesday**	Tuesdays	Tuesday's child
13.	**glue**	glues	glued	gluing
14.	(Am.) * **clue**	clues	clued	cluing
15.	(Br.) * **clew**	clews	clewed	clewing
16.	* **flue**	flues	flu	**thorough**
17.	* **flew**	It chased its tail.	It's mine.	They're all **through**.
18.	* **flu**	It's theirs.	although	That's too much.
19.	**influenza**	influenza	pursuit	pursuits
20.	**sue**	sues	sued	suing
21.	pursue	pursues	pursued	pursuing
22.	**true**	truly	pursuer	pursuers
23.	* **due**	duly	dues	duly
24.	undue	unduly	truthful	truly
25.	* **dew**	truth	overdue	avenue

* **Homophones**:

clew/clue   The British detective looked for a clew. The American, for a clue.

flew/flu/flue   What do you call a chimney disease? The flue flu.

What happened when the chimney exploded? The flue flew.

What happened when the chimney disease went away? The flue flu flew away.

do/due/dew   What are you going to do when the dew is due?

See the complete -oast family on p. 235 in *The Patterns of English Spelling* (TPES); -ity, p. 729; -ue, p. 314.

	157th day	158th day	159th day	160th day
1.	* **cue**	cues	cued	cuing
2.	**rescue**	rescues	rescued	rescuing
3.	barbecue	barbecues	rescuer	rescuers
4.	**argue**	argues	**argued**	**arguing**
5.	**value**	values	valued	valuing
6.	**valuable**	valuables	continuous	continuously
7.	**continue**	continues	continued	continuing
8.	* **hue**	hues	continual	continually
9.	discontinue	discontinues	discontinued	discontinuing
10.	* **Hugh**	Mr. Hughes	**although**	**though**
11.	* **queue**	queues	queued	queuing
12.	**statue**	statues	**through**	**thoroughly**
13.	**virtue**	virtues	virtuous	virtuously
14.	**issue**	issues	issued	issuing
15.	**tissue**	tissues	argument	argumentative
16.	**suit**	suits	suited	suiting
17.	pursuit	pursuits	suitable	suitably
18.	**fruit**	fruits	fruited	**It's too good.**
19.	**body**	bodies	full-bodied	**You're right.**
20.	**anybody**	somebody	nobody	**everybody**
21.	**antibody**	antibodies	student	studious
22.	**study**	**studies**	**studied**	**studying**
23.	darken	darkens	darkened	darkening
24.	blacken	blackens	blackened	blackening
25.	burden	burdens	burdened	burdening

* **Homophones**:

cue/queue   What do you call a line formed to buy pool sticks? A cue queue.

Hugh/hue/hew   Hugh knows how to hew wood and can tell what each hue of wood means.

See the complete -ue family on p. 314 in *The Patterns of English Spelling* (TPES); -uit, p. 429; -body, p. 711; -en, pp. 857-860.

Evaluation Test #4
(After 160 Days)

		Pattern Being Tested	Lesson word is in
1.	What is the ch**eapest** shot you've ever heard?	eapest	111
2.	We have succ**eeded** where others have failed.	eeded	111
3.	The lemonade needs some extra sw**eetening**.	eetening	116
4.	We were sl**ightly** late for church.	ightly	116
5.	Look what the cat br**ought** in! A dead mouse!	ought	117
6.	Both my d**aughters** are married and have careers.	aughters	118
7.	Sometimes you need recomm**endations** to get a job.	endations	124
8.	Diamond rings can be very, very exp**ensive**.	ensive	124
9.	I wish you would stop pret**ending** to be an expert.	ending	123
10.	What was Juliet doing up on the balc**ony**?	ony	125
11.	Nobody likes to be overl**ooked**.	ooked	130
12.	We were w**orried** about you.	orried	135
13.	Has it ever occ**urred** to you that you might be wrong?	urred	135
14.	Smoking is haz**ardous** to your health.	ardous	140
15.	I think you need some more inf**ormation** before you go.	ormation	144
16.	I wish you would stop squ**irming** in your seat.	irming	144
17.	I hope you have l**earned** your lesson.	earned	147
18.	Nothing quenches your th**irst** like water.	irst	149
19.	Jack is always b**oasting** about how good he is.	oasting	156
20.	This test will be contin**ued** tomorrow. Just kidding.	ued	159

	161st day	162nd day	163rd day	164th day
1.	sadden	saddens	saddened	saddening
2.	madden	maddens	maddened	maddening
3.	thicken	thickens	thickened	thickening
4.	**open**	**opens**	**opened**	**opening**
5.	**happen**	**happens**	**happened**	**happening**
6.	sicken	sickens	sickened	sickening
7.	**loosen**	loosens	**loosened**	loosening
8.	**tighten**	tightens	**tightened**	tightening
9.	threaten	threatens	**threatened**	**threatening**
10.	**listen**	**listens**	**listened**	**listening**
12.	**fasten**	fastens	**fastened**	fastening
13.	fastener	fasteners	brightener	brighteners
14.	brighten	brightens	brightened	brightening
15.	sweeten	sweetens	sweetened	sweetening
16.	listener	listeners	sweetener	sweeteners
17.	moisten	moistens	moistened	moistening
18.	fatten	fattens	fattened	fattening
19.	christen	christens	christened	christening
20.	glisten	glistens	glistened	glistening
21.	**soften**	softens	softened	softening
22.	softener	softeners	worse	worst
23.	**straighten**	straightens	straightened	straightening
24.	worse	worst	lightning bug	bolt of lightning
25.	lighten	lightens	lightened	lightening

See the complete -en family on pp. 857-860 in *The Patterns of English Spelling* (TPES).

	165th day	166th day	167th day	168th day
1.	picket	pickets	picketed	picketing
2.	**ticket**	tickets	ticketed	ticketing
3.	**pocket**	pockets	pocketed	pocketing
4.	**rocket**	rockets	rocketed	rocketing
5.	cricket	crickets	thicket	thickets
6.	socket	sockets	bucket	buckets
7.	**jacket**	jackets	sprocket	sprockets
8.	**blanket**	blankets	blanketed	blanketing
9.	**market**	markets	marketed	marketing
10.	trinket	trinkets	junket	junkets
11.	**basket**	baskets	casket	caskets
12.	gasket	gaskets	brisket	We're not through.
13.	* **racket**	rackets	racketeer	racketeers
14.	bracket	brackets	packet	packets
15.	**target**	targets	targeted	targeting
16.	**budget**	budgets	budgeted	budgeting
17.	fidget	fidgets	fidgeted	fidgeting
18.	midget	midgets	fussbudget	fussbudgets
19.	wind can ** **buffet**	the wind buffets	we were buffeted	buffeting
20.	a ** **buffet** dinner	buffet style	open buffet	tasty buffet
21.	**diet**	diets	dieted	dieting
22.	**quiet**	quiets	quieted	quieting
23.	**quietly**	tablet	tablets	goblet
24.	toilet	toilets	toiletries	poems
25.	**poet**	poets	**poetry**	poetic

* **Homophones**:

racket/racquet   What do you call the making of tennis equipment? The racquet racket.

* **Heteronyms**:

buffet ("buh FAY") / buffet ("BUF it")   You can go to a buffet dinner. The wind can buffet you.

See the complete -et family on p. 685 in *The Patterns of English Spelling* (TPES).

	169th day	170th day	171st day	172nd day
1.	anklet	anklets	skillet	skillets
2.	booklet	booklets	wallet	wallets
3.	bullet	bullets	Hamlet	hamlets
4.	violet	violets	couplet	couplets
5.	comet	comets	bonnet	bonnets
6.	**planet**	planets	planetary	planetarium
7.	muppet	muppets	puppet	puppets
8.	**carpet**	carpets	trumpet	trumpets
9.	interpret	interprets	interpreted	interpreting
10.	interpreter	interpreters	interpretation	misinterpreting
11.	**closet**	**closets**	closeted	closeting
12.	rivet	rivets	riveted	riveting
13.	covet	covets	coveted	coveting
14.	velvet	velveteen	suet	crumpets
15.	sonnet	sonnets	cabinet	cabinets
16.	* **racquet**	racquets	goblet	goblets
17.	* **racket**	rackets	turret	turrets
18.	bracelet	bracelets	triplet	triplets
19.	* **prophet**	prophets	nugget	nuggets
20.	musket	muskets	musketeer	musketeers
21.	omelet	omelets	ringlet	ringlets
22.	pamphlet	pamphlets	mallet	mallets
23.	inlet	inlets	helmet	helmets
24.	banquet	banquets	tourniquet	tourniquets
25.	garret	garrets	Margaret	Margaret's

* Homophones:

racket/racquet   What do you call the making of tennis equipment? The racquet racket.

prophet/profit   What do you call money made from predictions? Prophet profit.

See the complete -et family on p. 685 in *The Patterns of English Spelling* (TPES).

	173rd day	174th day	175th day	176th day
1.	ought	fought	bought	ought to
2.	**thought**	thoughts	thoughtful	thoughtfulness
3.	bought	brought	brought	brought
4.	brought	thoughtless	thoughtlessness	thoughtfully
5.	**though**	**thoroughly**	They're all **through**.	We're not **through**.
6.	**although**	thoroughness	**thoroughly**	thoroughness
7.	succeed	succeeds	succeeded	succeeding
8.	**success**	successes	successful	successfully
9.	profess	professor	profession	professional
10.	depress	depressed	depression	depressions
11.	**discuss**	discussed	discussing	discussions
12.	**skipping**	skipper	skipped	skips
13.	**whips**	whipped	whippings	whipping
14.	**crush**	crushed	crushing	crushes
15.	**splash**	splashed	splashing	splashes
16.	**remember**	remembers	remembered	remembering
17.	grumble	grumbled	grumbles	grumbling
18.	swindle	swindled	swindlers	swindling
19.	**branch**	branches	branched	branching
20.	**stretch**	stretched	stretchers	stretches
21.	lecture	lectures	lectured	lecturing
22.	**picture**	pictures	pictured	picturing
23.	**crutch**	crutches	warned	warnings
24.	**daughter**	two daughters	my daughter's friend	It's too hard
25.	**laughter**	laughing	laughed	laughs

See the complete -ought family on p. 117 in *The Patterns of English Spelling* (TPES); -ough, p. 214; -eed, p. 402; -ess, p. 157; -uss, p. 160; -ip, p. 128; -ash, p. 209; -ush, p. 211; -mber, p.639; -mble, p. 606; -nch, pp. 206-207; -etch, p. 202; -cture, p. 923; utch, p. 205; -aughter, p. 430.

Sequential Spelling Level 3 - Teacher's Guide

	177th day	178th day	179th day	180th day
1.	**preach**	preaches	preachers	preaching
2.	**double**	doubles	**doubled**	**doubling**
3.	**trouble**	troubles	**troubled**	**troubling**
4.	**award**	awards	awarded	awarding
5.	**reward**	rewarded	rewarding	rewards
6.	**dwarf**	dwarfs	dwarfed	dwarfing
7.	**touch**	touches	untouched	touching
8.	swatch	swatches	watchful	watchfulness
9.	**flight**	slightly	unsightly	lightest
10.	**defend**	defended	defending	defenders
11.	**befriend**	befriended	friendly	friendliness
12.	**rainy**	tiny	tiniest	shiny
13.	crony	cronies	corny	corniest
14.	corny	cornier	**corniest**	**proof**
15.	**prove**	proves	**proved**	**proving**
16.	**remove**	removes	**removed**	**removal**
17.	**approve**	approves	**approved**	**approval**
18.	**marry**	married	**marries**	**marrying**
19.	**hurry**	hurried	**hurries**	**hurrying**
20.	**occur**	occurs	**occurred**	**occurring**
21.	**standard**	afterwards	cowardly	hazard
22.	**confirm**	squirming	affirm	affirmative
23.	**conform**	performing	transformer	forest
24.	**sharpening**	sharpened	thirsty	interesting
25.	**continued**	continuing	barbecue	rescuers

See the complete -each family on p. 437 in *The Patterns of English Spelling* (TPES); -war-, p. 502; -ight, p. 428; -ny, p. 718-19; -ove, p. 326; -rry, p. 706; -ur, p. 520; -ard, p. 506; -irm, p.515; -orm, p. 517; -ue, p. 314.

FINAL EVALUATION TEST

		Pattern being tested	Lesson word is in
1.	I hope we don't have another depr**ession**.	ession	4
2.	We'll have a group disc**ussion** tomorrow.	ussion	4
3.	I love going to wedding rec**eptions**.	eptions	16
4.	We were really **worried** about you.	worried	27
5.	My cousin sk**ipped** the fourth grade.	ipped	35
6.	We were simply cr**ushed** to find we weren't invited.	ushed	39
7.	My sister is taking up acc**ounting** in college.	ounting	52
8.	I sometimes have to be rem**inded** about the time.	inded	63
9.	It's no fun to be mar**ooned** on a desert island.	ooned	67
10.	I wish they would stop gr**umbling** all the time.	umbling	72
11.	They had to trim several br**anches** off the tree.	anches	78
12.	The injured player was carried out on a str**etcher**.	etcher	88
13.	The player suffered a fr**acture**.	acture	89
14.	Do you remember who st**arred** in Gone With the Wind?	arred	103
15.	When I hurt my foot, I had to walk on cr**utches**.	utches	106
16.	We have succ**eeded** where others have failed.	eeded	111
17.	Both my d**aughters** are married and have careers.	aughters	118
18.	Has it ever occ**urred** to you that you might be wrong.	urred	135
19.	I hope you have l**earned** your lesson.	earned	147
20.	Jill is always b**oasting** about how good she is.	oasting	156
21.	What's h**appening**?	appening	164
22.	I wish people were better l**isteners** than talkers.	isteners	162
23.	We are on a really tight b**udget**.	udget	165
24.	My cousin plays the tr**umpet**.	umpet	171
25.	I hate being called in and put on the c**arpet**.	arpet	169

Answer Key

Day 3
Unscramble these
1. lsycas **classy**
2. ysgas **gassy**
3. sfarsasas **sassafras**
4. sdeaps **passed**
5. bassruleg **bluegrass**
6. duesges **guessed**
7. cseuslfcus **successful**
8. pesosorfr **professor**
9. ciesnsongf **confessing**
10. idgpenesrs **depressing**

Day 4

```
S + M + + + + + C N P + G + +
D R + A + + + L O + R + N + +
+ E E + S + A I + G O + I U +
+ + P S + S S + N + C + S N +
+ + + R S S I I + L E + S L +
+ + + I E A S N E + S S E E +
+ + E C + S P S G + S E R S +
+ S C + E + S S + + E S D S +
T U + R + E + I E + D S + + +
S + P + R + + + O R + A + + +
C O N F E S S I O N T L + + +
E N I L O S A G + + + G + + +
G A S S I N G + + + + E + + +
+ + + + + + + + + + + Y + + +
+ + + + + + + + + + + E + + +
```

(Over, Down, Direction)
CLASSIEST(9,1,SW)
CONFESSION(1,11,E)
DEPRESSION(1,2,SE)
DRESSING(13,8,N)
EYEGLASSES(12,15,N)
GASOLINE(8,12,W)
GASSING(1,13,E)
LESSER(10,5,SW)
MASSING(3,1,SE)
PRESSING(3,10,NE)
PROCESSED(11,1,S)
SUCCESSION(1,10,NE)
TRESPASSERS(11,11,NW)
UNLESS(14,3,S)

Day 5
Fill in the blank:
1. **Stress** can cause health problems such as high blood pressure.
2. When I drove my brother to the airport, I gave him a goodbye **kiss**.
3. Jack needs to leave at least ten minutes earlier or he'll **miss** the bus.
4. The judge will **dismiss** the jury soon.
5. We need to **discuss** what to do about this.
6. What's all the **fuss** about?
7. The builders are making **progress** on the house.
8. The SS Edmund Fitzgerald never sent a **distress** call before it sank in November 1975.
9. Lisa tried to **impress** Jon with her knowledge of football but she failed miserably.
10. Brian isn't very good at soccer; **nevertheless** he keeps trying!

Day 9
Fill in the blank:
1. Who's the **best** player on the team?
2. The baby robins are just about ready to leave the **nest**.
3. What do you **suggest** I study so I can pass the **test**?
4. Lots of people attended the meeting to **protest** the tax increase.
5. Sally tugged at her brother's **sleeve** to get his attention.
6. Did you **ever** see such a beautiful sight? It's gorgeous!
7. She pulled the **lever** to release the balloons.
8. How much time do we need to **invest** in this effort?
9. Babies need food that is easy to **digest**.
10. Jack and Sam stopped to **rest** on their way home.

Day 10
Unscramble these:
1. ttessde **detests**
2. eporttss **protests**
3. ggstuess **suggests**
4. gdtescnoe **congested**
5. ehaerwtv **whatever**
6. ensistf **infests**
7. eesvnla **leavens**
8. leenev **eleven**
9. seerdev **severed**
10. vrhweeo **however**

Day 12

```
+ + + + + + + + + + + + + + +
+ + G + + + + + + + + + + + L
+ W N D I G E S T I O N + U +
S H I R T S L E E V E S F + C
+ E T + E N U + R + + I + O +
+ R S + V E + G + E T + N + E
+ E E + E V A + G U V G + V +
+ V T + N A + R A E E E E + S
+ E O + T E + E R S S N O E +
+ R R + U H B + T E I T V H +
+ + P + A + + I + N S E I + W
+ + + + L + O + G + E T + O +
+ + + + L N + + + P + + I + N
+ + + + Y T N E M T S E V N I
+ + L A R E V E S + + + + + G
```

(Over,Down,Direction)
ARRESTING(7,7,SE)
BEAUTIFUL(7,10,NE)
CONGESTION(15,4,SW)
DIGESTION(4,3,E)
EVENING(15,6,SW)
EVENTUALLY(5,5,S)
HEAVENS(6,10,N)
INVESTMENT(15,14,W)
PEEVES(10,13,NE)
PROTESTING(3,11,N)
SEVERAL(9,15,W)
SHIRTSLEEVES(1,4,E)
SUGGESTION(6,4,SE)
WHEREVER(2,3,S)
WHOEVER(15,11,NW)

Day 13

Fill in the blank

1. Sam and Rob helped catch the **thief**.
2. After such a bumpy ride, it was a **relief** to get off the plane.
3. At the memorial service, many people were overcome with **grief**.
4. What time do you want to **leave** for home?
5. Did you **receive** the gift I sent you?
6. Alison didn't study for the **quiz**, but she took it anyway.
7. Brian is a **whiz** at video games.
8. His waving **handkerchief** attracted my attention.
9. Early explorers held the **belief** that the earth was flat.
10. Emily is easy to **deceive** because she is so trusting.

Day 14

1. ehvtise **thieves**
2. bivleese **believes**
3. dprnioveeecc **preconceived**
4. veepierc **perceives**
5. eeecrivs **receives**
6. heeasv **heaves**
7. wezszhi **whizzes**
8. ibedsefr **debriefs**
9. eecshvai **achieves**
10. vgeiser **grieves**

Day 18

Fill in the blank:

1. Don't you just love these **fuzzy** slippers? They're so comfortable!
2. Jackie really likes to work on crossword **puzzles**.
3. My sister **suffers** from diabetes.
4. Let's hope that putting cotton in our ears **stifles** the noise when they shoot their rifles.
5. When my dog meets strangers, he always **sniffs** them.
6. Before he got in the patrol car, the policeman put the **handcuffs** on his prisoner.
7. We took a walk along the **cliffs** yesterday afternoon.
8. All of the county **sheriffs** in the state are meeting next week.
9. **Doesn't** she look like Emily's twin?
10. I really couldn't see the fire, just **puffs** of smoke.

Day 19

Unscramble these

1. csiehmif **mischief**
2. stmaffi **mastiff**
3. zzdmelu **muzzled**
4. fudeft **stuffed**
5. cfefusd **scuffed**
6. fuebfld **bluffed**
7. rfsfedeu **suffered**
8. ebudzz **buzzed**
9. feifsdn **sniffed**
10. wiedfhf **whiffed**

Day 22

Fill in the blank by using *they're*, *their* or *there*.

1. Where are Mark and Sally? **They're** over there.
2. They've forgotten **their** bags.
3. **There** is no soap in the bathroom. Could you bring some please?
4. **There** are several mistakes in this paper.
5. I've met them before, but I don't know **their** names.
6. I don't know who they are, but I think **they're** German.
7. Look at the smiles on **their** faces.
8. I don't think **they're** coming.
9. **There** are two reasons why I don't like this idea.
10. Where are Fred and Steve? Over **there**.

Day 24

1. igrnai **airing**
2. niaigrp **pairing**
3. fnruyila **unfairly**
4. iipaemntrm **impairment**
5. autsipsr **upstairs**
6. wadeernru **underwear**
7. aeirngb **bearing**
8. srseehi **heiress**
9. ibnrga **baring**
10. nuqsarig **squaring**

Day 25

Fill in the blank

1. The airlines just announced another **fare** increase.
2. Emily and Susan volunteered to **prepare** lunch.
3. Before it sank, the ship sent up a **flare**.
4. When we walk to school, we go past a house that has a sign on the gate "**beware**" of the dog.
5. We took the **silverware** to an appraiser to get an idea of its **worth**.
6. I'm always amazed by the view of the **world** from outer space.
7. Mr. Smith's students were asked to **compare** and contrast the Eastern United States and the Western United States.
8. Don't **worry**, the rain will stop soon.
9. During the Great Depression, **work** was **scarce**.
10. How many **workers** do we need to finish painting the house today?

Day 26

Unscramble these

1. earfs **fares**
2. rpeearsp **prepares**
3. cclaresy **scarcely**
4. redoewdr **reworded**
5. bolekawr **workable**
6. caorwkoe **cookware**
7. aeirarf **airfare**
8. aerws **wares**
9. wmiseroor **worrisome**
10. fworeksir **fireworks**

Sequential Spelling Level 3 - Teacher's Guide

Day 28

```
+  +  F  +  E  +  +  T  +  +  +  R  P  T  +
+  +  +  O  +  R  A  +  +  +  A  +  A  O  +
+  +  +  +  R  P  A  +  +  R  +  +  S  O  S
+  +  +  +  E  E  E  W  E  +  +  +  S  F  N
+  +  +  W  +  R  W  L  T  S  R  O  W  E  A
+  G  O  +  A  +  Y  O  G  F  +  +  O  R  R
+  R  L  W  +  +  +  N  R  +  O  +  R  A  I
M  +  A  A  +  +  I  +  +  D  +  S  D  B  N
G  N  I  Y  R  R  O  W  +  +  +  +  +  +  G
U  +  +  +  A  I  +  W  O  R  D  I  N  G  +
+  +  +  P  +  +  N  +  +  +  +  +  +  +  +
+  +  E  +  +  +  G  +  +  +  +  +  +  +  +
+  R  +  +  +  +  +  +  +  +  +  +  +  +  +
P  +  +  +  +  +  +  +  +  +  +  +  +  +  +
+  C  O  M  P  A  R  I  N  G  +  +  +  +  +
```

(Over, Down, Direction)

BAREFOOT(14,8,N)	SNARING(15,3,S)
COMPARING(2,15,E)	SOFTWARE(12,8,NW)
FOREWORD(3,1,SE)	TAPEWORM(8,1,SW)
GLARING(2,6,SE)	UNAWARE(1,10,NE)
PASSWORD(13,1,S)	WORDING(8,10,E)
PREPARING(1,14,NE)	WORRYING(8,9,W)
RARELY(12,1,SW)	WORST(13,5,W)

Day 29

Fill in the blank

1. The polo shirts come in several sizes; small, medium, **large** and extra-**large**.
2. Sam hooked up the car's battery to give it a **charge**.
3. The doctor said he would **discharge** my sister from the hospital today.
4. In order to replace the pipe, the plumber had to **enlarge** the opening.
5. There's nothing better than a good **soup** on a cold day.
6. Brian and Max will join the tour **group** in Rome next week.
7. The balloon deflated because of a small **rip** in the cloth.
8. Susan walked carefully over the broken sidewalk so she wouldn't **trip**.
9. Sometimes, jockeys use a **whip** to urge their horses to run faster.
10. Watch out! You don't want to **slip** on that icy sidewalk.

Day 31

Fill in the blank

1. mganeletner **enlargement**
2. grscahgiidn **discharging**
3. rgelar **larger**
4. cduepreo **recouped**
5. uonpoc **coupon**
6. dieppr **ripped**
7. irpetpd **tripped**
8. ihewpdp **whipped**
9. gnmliaar **marginal**
10. pysou **soupy**

Day 34

Fill in the blank

1. **Gypsies** are groups of people who don't stay in one place very long.
2. There were lots of **ships** in the harbor today.
3. Lisa bought a beautiful bunch of pink **tulips** for her grandmother.
4. Nancy helped her brother John get his jacket **unzipped**.
5. **Parsnips** are a root vegetable.
6. Many older homes have **copper** pipes.
7. Would you please make ten **copies** of this letter?
8. Our family's hardware store sells **mops** and brooms as well as nails.
9. We heard a **popping** sound before the explosion.
10. Jack wants to ride in a **spaceship** someday.

Day 35

Unscramble these

1. rippez **zipper**
2. ygdppe **gypped**
3. pperhwsdoi **worshipped**
4. phrdashi **hardship**
5. pohped **hopped**
6. veroprp **proper**
7. petspro **stopper**
8. pciroe **copier**
9. ghpnipoc **chopping**
10. pogigsnsi **gossiping**

Day 37

Fill in the blank

1. As fish sizes go, that one's a real **whopper**.
2. Jake worked **nonstop** to finish his paper before the deadline.
3. It isn't polite to **eavesdrop** on a private conversation.
4. One of Max's chores is to take out the **trash** on Fridays.
5. I have to stop at the bank and get some **cash** for the movie.
6. Kristin would like to study **fashion** in New York City.
7. Shrimp is part of the **shellfish** family.
8. I **wish** I hadn't broken that **dish**.
9. Don't forget to **brush** your teeth.
10. Some people **blush** easily. Are you one of them?

Day 41

1. We waited for the tow truck to give us a **push**.
2. The **bush** we planted last spring is growing very well.
3. How many apples are in a **bushel**?
4. There's the bell. There's someone at the **door**.
5. The Salvation Army is one of the organizations that collects money for the **poor**.
6. We made reservations for **four** at the restaurant.
7. Please **pour** me a glass of lemonade.
8. A **boor** is someone who is rude and has no manners.
9. Did you remember to sweep the **floor** after you spilled the sugar?
10. A **metaphor** is a figure of speech.

Day 45
Fill in the blank
1. Are you coming to **our** house after school?
2. I need 2 cups of **flour** to make your birthday cake.
3. This milk has gone **sour**.
4. I'm going to take a course in **flower** arranging this spring.
5. Flipping a circuit breaker restores **power**.
6. Did you hear that car **horn**?
7. Let's pop some **corn** to take to the movie.
8. What year were you **born**?
9. Sirens are used to **warn** of approaching tornadoes.
10. I went to my sister's bridal **shower** last week.

Day 47
1. outhrgh **through**
2. truhgooh **thorough**
3. udreoevd **devoured**
4. derous **soured**
5. rpeooerwved **overpowered**
6. ncoyr **corny**
7. pnpcoor **popcorn**
8. denraw **warned**
9. lhhutago **although**
10. itfuebaul **beautiful**

Day 50
1. itrspmo **imports**
2. tsaoptrsnr **transports**
3. ssropatps **passports**
4. gdhoetisrtsh **shortsighted**
5. mantuso **amounts**
6. sucondsit **discounts**
7. psonrnuo **pronouns**
8. uoidtmsn **dismount**
9. dedrotpe **deported**
10. rtpspsou **supports**

Day 51
Fill in the blank
1. We borrowed a **portable** heater to keep warm.
2. After arriving at the airport, our tour group was **transported** to our hotel in a bus.
3. My mom and I **sorted** through family pictures last weekend.
4. Our house doesn't have a garage; it has a **carport**.
5. **Although** it was raining, Jack still wanted to ride his bike.
6. Do you know a **shortcut** to the store?
7. How do you **pronounce** that word?
8. Mount McKinley is the highest **mountain** in North America.
9. Adam and Emma **counted** the votes for class president.
10. With so many cousins living nearby, we don't have a **shortage** of playmates.

Day 52

```
A E S + N + R E + + + + + D T
N V + E + O G E + + + + E + R
N I + + I A I + P + + C + + O
O T + + T T + T + O N + + + P
U R + R + + N + A U R + + + R
N O O + + + + U O T + T + + I
C P + + + + + N O + R + E + A
E P + + + + O + + C + O + R +
R U S H O R T B R E A D P + S
+ S E X P O R T I N G + + E +
N O I T A T R O P S N A R T D
G N I T R O C S E + + + + + +
+ + + + + + + + C O U N T Y +
+ + + + + + + + + + + + + + +
G N I T R O P M I + + + + + +
```

(Over,Down,Direction)
AIRPORT(15,7,N)
ANNOUNCER(1,1,S)
COUNTIES(10,8,NW)
COUNTY(9,13,E)
DEPORTATION(15,11,NW)
ESCORTING(9,12,W)
EXPORTING(3,10,E)

IMPORTING(9,15,W)
PORTAGE(2,7,NE)
PRONOUNCED(5,10,NE)
REPORTERS(7,1,SE)
SHORTBREAD(3,9,E)
SUPPORTIVE(2,10,N)
TRANSPORTATION(14,11,W)

Day 53
Fill in the blank
1. How much does an **ounce** of gold weigh?
2. The harder you **bounce** a ball, the higher it goes.
3. Did you see the cat **pounce** on the mouse?
4. You have pretty **brown** eyes!
5. Why such a nasty **frown**? What's wrong?
6. Chuckles the **clown** is coming to our **town**.
7. **Rich** people tend to drive expensive cars like Jaguars.
8. What's your favorite **sandwich**? Mine is corned beef and swiss on rye.
9. I think the shovel is under that **pile** of snow.
10. She's got a lovely **smile**.

Day 57
Fill in the blank
1. **While** we were sleeping, it started snowing.
2. Another name for a wastebasket is circular **file**.
3. It will take awhile to **compile** the list.
4. We decided to buy new **tile** for our kitchen floor.
5. There's a **hole** in the bucket that we need to fix.
6. I'm not sure if we can **reconcile** our differences.
7. What furniture **style** do you like better, traditional or contemporary?
8. Napoleon went into **exile** on the island of Elba
9. A **crocodile** is a **reptile** that is related to an alligator.
10. Peeking through the ship's **porthole** we saw palm trees and white sand.

Day 60

```
E  L  I  N  E  V  U  J  +  +  N  N  T  G  +
W  I  +  +  +  +  +  +  O  +  O  U  N  +
C  O  N  S  O  L  A  T  I  O  N  I  R  I  +
+  +  R  S  +  +  +  T  +  +  +  T  N  L  +
+  +  +  T  O  +  A  +  +  +  +  A  S  I  +
E  +  +  +  H  L  +  +  +  +  +  I  T  F  H
+  L  +  +  I  W  E  +  C  +  +  L  I  E  O
+  +  O  P  +  +  H  O  +  +  +  I  L  D  L
+  +  M  H  +  +  N  I  +  +  G  C  E  +  Y
+  O  +  +  P  S  +  +  L  N  +  N  S  +  +
C  +  +  +  O  O  +  +  I  E  +  O  +  +  +
+  +  +  L  +  W  O  L  +  +  +  C  +  +  +
+  +  +  I  +  I  +  Y  L  +  +  +  E  +  +
+  N  +  L  +  T  +  +  +  +  R  +  +  +
G  +  E  +  S  +  +  +  F  I  L  I  N  G  +
```

(Over, Down, Direction)
COMPILATION(1,11,NE)
CONSOLATION(1,3,E)
CONSOLING(9,7,SW)
DEFILING(14,8,N)
FILING(9,15,E)
HOLY(15,6,S)
INSOLE(2,2,SE)

JUVENILE(8,1,W)
LOOPHOLE(8,13,NW)
RECONCILIATION(12,14,N)
STYLING(5,15,NE)
TURNSTILES(13,1,S)
WILE(6,12,SW)
WORTHWHILE(1,2,SE)

Day 64

```
+  +  O  +  +  +  +  +  +  +  +  M  +  +  G
+  +  O  +  +  +  +  +  +  +  A  +  +  +  N
+  +  B  +  +  +  +  +  S  +  +  G  I
+  +  M  +  +  +  +  T  +  +  N  +  O
G  +  A  +  +  +  E  +  +  I  +  +  O
+  N  B  R  E  T  R  A  U  Q  D  N  I  H  P
+  +  I  +  +  M  +  +  N  +  T  A  +  M
W  I  N  D  I  E  S  T  I  H  A  +  L  A
+  +  +  N  N  G  +  W  +  T  G  +  T  +  H
+  +  D  +  N  I  E  +  O  +  +  U  H  +  S
+  E  +  I  +  R  C  O  +  +  +  O  +
D  +  O  +  +  +  I  S  +  +  +  U  H  +
+  O  +  +  +  N  +  E  +  +  +  G  +  T
B  +  +  +  G  +  +  +  R  +  +  H  +
+  +  +  +  G  N  I  O  O  H  S  +  +  +
```

(Over, Down, Direction)
ALTHOUGH(13,7,S)
BAMBOO(3,6,N)
BOOING(1,14,NE)
HINDQUARTER(14,6,W)
MASTERMINDED(12,1,SW)
RESCINDING(10,14,NW)

REWINDING(6,11,NE)
SHAMPOOING(15,10,N)
SHOOING(11,15,W)
TATOOING(12,7,SW)
THOUGH(15,13,NW)
WINDIEST(1,8,E)

Day 61

Fill in the blank

1. Do you **mind** if I sit here?
2. Please **remind** me to get bread at the grocery store.
3. A white cane is often used by someone who is **blind**.
4. It was **kind** of you to include us in your dinner plans.
5. Do you need to **wind** the clock? It seems to be slowing down.
6. The **wind** is blowing very hard. It's making the trees bend.
7. **Whirlwind** is another name for tornado or cyclone.
8. The judge told the sheriff to **rescind** the order.
9. I got burned by a **cinder** because I stood too close to the fire.
10. The frost made beautiful patterns on the **window**.

Day 66

1. At summer camp, we learned how to paddle **canoes**.
2. During the Great Depression, my dad worked as a **shoe-shine** boy.
3. Have you ever played the game of **horseshoes**.
4. How many **moons** does Jupiter have?
5. On Saturday mornings, Jack likes to watch **cartoons**.
6. Tip, which hit southern Japan in October 1979, was the largest and most intense **typhoon** on record.
7. A pirate's loot is called **booty**.
8. These **bootie** socks are warm and cozy.
9. Bill spent several hours **troubleshooting** the problem before he solved it.
10. Cowboys in the Old West liked to visit the **saloons** on Saturday nights.

Day 67

1. ndocea **canoed**
2. ehods **shoed**
3. ooomynhne **honeymoon**
4. obodlelan **ballooned**
5. newsood **swooned**
6. utootho **shootout**
7. huretblsertooor **troubleshooter**
8. toaneops **teaspoon**
9. poontno **pontoon**
10. stancoirto **cartoonist**

Day 68

```
N B + G + + + + T + B + S + R
O + A + N + + E + S O + N O +
O + + B + I A + E + O + O N +
C + + + O S N C + + T T W O +
C + + + P O A O + + I + S O +
A + + O + L N + O N N + H P +
R + O + E + + S G T G + O S +
S N O O M Y E N O H R + E E G
+ + H N O O T T I P S A S L N
+ S A F T E R N O O N + C B I
C A N O E I N G + + + + + A T
R E T O O C S + + + + + + T O
+ + + + + + + + + + + + + T O
+ + + + + + + + + + + + + + O
+ + + + + + + + + + + + + + H
+ + + + + + + + + + + + + + S
```

(Over,Down,Direction)

AFTERNOON(3,10,E)	ROOTING(15,1,SW)
BABOONS(2,1,SE)	SCOOTER(7,12,W)
BOOTING(11,1,S)	SHOELACES(2,10,NE)
CANOEING(1,11,E)	SHOOTING(15,15,N)
CARTOONING(13,10,NW)	SNOWSHOES(13,1,S)
HONEYMOONS(10,8,W)	SPITTOON(11,9,W)
RACCOON(1,7,N)	TABLESPOON(14,12,N)
	TEASPOON(9,1,SW)

Day 70

Fill in the blank:

1. When I dance, I have two left **feet**.
2. Mountain goats are very **surefooted** on steep hillsides.
3. Ballroom dancers have to practice their **footwork**.
4. Let's see if she **remembers** the trip.
5. We will grow **cucumbers** and squash in our garden this year.
6. I hope I don't **stumble** over my words.
7. We heard several **grumbles** about the change in plans.
8. There were some **rumbles** of thunder before the storm came.
9. The cabin at the lake has large **timbers** supporting the roof.
10. The **members** of the committee asked Jake to be the chair.

Day 71

1. oorhluhtgy **thoroughly**
2. ugohhtal **although**
3. hmispeemrb **membership**
4. emrmdbeeer **remembered**
5. belmdire **limbered**
6. ucdneemreb **encumbered**
7. oebbrm **bomber**
8. blrcemi **climber**
9. nobdteeuurm **outnumbered**
10. muegbldr **grumbled**

Day 75

Fill in the blank:

1. I'm sorry for the **misunderstanding**.
2. A symbol of Zeus is the **thunderbolt**.
3. We **bundled** up in our winter coats and went outside to go sledding.
4. The crowd **dwindled** steadily after the fire was put out.
5. We are **hunting** for a house on the lake.
6. Ron **mishandled** his reaction to his critics.
7. Red, white and blue **bunting** is used on the Fourth of July.
8. The prison escape caused a large **manhunt**.
9. The pigs **grunted** as they played in the mud.
10. The store clerk **handled** the china with care.

Day 76

```
+ + + S R E T N U H + + + + +
+ U G N I L D N I W D + + T +
N + N + K + + + + + + R + R +
+ O + D + I + + + + E + U +
+ + I + E + N + + T + + N G
D O O T S R E D N U S I M D N
S G + + A + W U L + + G + L I
R R + + + T H E B I O + + I T
E U + + + D N L N D N + + N N
L N + + A + U O R T + G + G O
D T + E + N + E R + + + + + R
N I H + T + D + + F + + + + F
I N B L U N D E R I N G + + N
W G Y + U + + + + + + O + + O
S H A N D L I N G + + + C + C
```

(Over,Down,Direction)

BLUNDERING(3,13,E)	HEADHUNTER(3,12,NE)
BLUNTLY(9,8,SW)	HUNTERS(10,1,W)
CONFRONTATION(13,15,NW)	KINDLING(5,3,SE)
CONFRONTING(15,15,N)	MISUNDERSTOOD(13,6,W)
DWINDLING(11,2,W)	SWINDLERS(1,15,N)
GRUNTING(2,7,S)	TRUNDLING(14,2,S)
HANDLING(2,15,E)	UNDERDOG(5,14,NE)
	UNDERWENT(2,2,SE)

Day 78

1. ucsleanh **launches**
2. nsukams **unmasks**
3. ssbak **basks**
4. wshski **whisks**
5. anhsecr **ranches**
6. ucanhesh **haunches**
7. sushk **husks**
8. layuetbfliu **beautifully**
9. brsecnah **branches**
10. kflssa **flasks**

Day 79
Fill in the blank:
1. I filled the **basket** with tomatoes.
2. Janice **asked** if she could borrow my bike.
3. Sam worked with the reporters at the **news desk**.
4. Lisa **whisked** the eggs into the batter.
5. The policeman **frisked** the suspect.
6. Susan **husked** the corn for supper.
7. Alison **thoroughly** cleaned her room before leaving on a trip.
8. The rocket was **launched** yesterday.
9. The garden club is taking responsibility for **beautifying** Main Street.
10. The trail **branched** in many different directions.

Day 81
Fill in the blank
1. I didn't **flinch** when I felt her **pinch**.
2. Did you see the **finch** outside the window?
3. What a lovely **bunch** of daffodils!
4. I have a **hunch** that it will rain tonight.
5. What did you bring to **munch** on for **lunch**?
6. Please hand me the pipe **wrench**. It's on the work**bench**.
7. Water helps **quench** a thirst.
8. He landed a **punch** before falling down.
9. Did you hear the **crunch** of gravel?
10. It rained heavily **throughout** the state this week.

Day 82
1. hreencws   **wrenches**
2. ehbnsec   **benches**
3. eusehnqc   **quenches**
4. htrhyglouo   **thoroughly**
5. snhect   **stench**
6. yclhsen   **lynches**
7. lhcefsni   **flinches**
8. csrnhuecs   **scrunches**
9. eucsnrhb   **brunches**
10. ecrunhcs   **crunches**

Day 84
```
+ + + + + + + D G + + + + + S
F + + + + Q U E N C H I N G E
A L T H O U G H I + + + + + I
+ + I + + + C H + + + + G H
+ + + N + + + N C + + + N + C
G + C + C + + E N + + I + W N
+ N L T + H + R Y + H + W I U
+ + I + H + I T L C + E + N M
+ + N H + O + N N + D + + C +
+ + C + C + U E G N + + + H +
+ + H + + N R G E + + + + I +
+ + I + + W E S H + + + + N +
+ + N + + + D B + + + + + G +
+ + G + + A S N O E H C N U L
+ + + + + Y P I N C H I N G + +
```

(Over, Down, Direction)
ALTHOUGH(1,3,E)
BENCHING(8,13,NW)
CLINCHING(3,6,S)
ENTRENCHED(8,10,N)
FLINCHING(1,2,SE)
LUNCHEONS(15,14,W)
LYNCHING(9,8,N)
MUNCHIES(15,8,N)
PINCHING(6,15,E)
QUENCHING(6,2,E)
THOUGH(4,7,SE)
WEDNESDAY(13,7,SW)
WINCHING(14,6,S)
WRENCHING(6,12,NE)

Day 86
1. ucchesrh   **churches**
2. ehsculr   **lurches**
3. rcheesp   **perches**
4. tecetharas   **reattaches**
5. isdthascep   **dispatches**
6. esabcht   **batches**
7. ehsstcacr   **scratches**
8. htrcwees   **wretches**
9. ksetsech   **sketches**
10. fcshtee   **fetches**

Day 91
Fill in the blank:
1. Emily asked Kristin if she would be a **bridesmaid**.
2. Jack and Sam **switched** places so Sam could sit next to Alison.
3. Brian practiced **pitching** with Adam.
4. **Which** of the two desserts do you like better?
5. Mr. Ellison **lectured** the class about the Middle Ages.
6. Many textiles are **manufactured** in South Carolina.
7. I **honestly** don't know what happened!
8. Walter Cronkite was a famous **broadcaster** for CBS News.
9. Luke fell and **fractured** his ankle.
10. Katie **braided** Annie's hair.

Day 92
```
S + + + + + + + + + + G N +
A B G N I R U T C E L N + E +
N + E + + + + + + + I + + H +
D + + W + + + + + R + + S C +
W + + + I + + + U + + W + T +
I + + + + T + T M + I G G I +
C B R O A D C A S T I N G K +
H + + + H A I H C + I I + + H
E + + C F D + H I H + R + + O
S + I U E + I + C N + U + + N
+ H N N + N + T + + G T + + E
W A S + G + I + W I T C H E S
M + + + + + + + + + + + I + + T
S R E D I A R + + + + + P + + Y
+ + + + + + + + + + + + + + +
```

65

Continued from Day 92

(Over,Down,Direction)
BEWITCHING(2,2,SE)
BROADCASTING(2,7,E)
HONESTY(15,8,S)
ITCHING(7,12,NE)
KITCHEN(14,7,N)
LECTURING(11,2,W)
MAIDENS(9,6,SW)

MANUFACTURING(1,13,NE)
PICTURING(12,14,N)
RAIDERS(7,14,W)
SANDWICHES(1,1,S)
SWITCHING(13,4,SW)
WHICH(1,12,NE)
WITCHES(9,12,E)

Day 93
Fill in the blank:
1. Here's the **key** for the door.
2. Did you see that **monkey**? He's cute!
3. How much **money** do we need for the trip?
4. **They** are planning a trip to New Zealand this month.
5. Lisa discovered several **grey** hairs yesterday.
6. Large animals **prey** on smaller animals.
7. My dog is learning to **obey** my commands.
8. I made enough cupcakes for **each** of us to have one.
9. Chemicals have to be stored safely so they don't **leach** into the soil.
10. **Hey**! Let's go swimming!

Day 97
1. ahrce **reach**
2. ecaht **teach**
3. ephacr **preach**
4. eerbch **breech**
5. pcehse **speech**
6. elbean **enable**
7. saildeb **disable**
8. dlebou **double**
9. urbtelo **trouble**
10. sebtal **stable**

Day 99

```
+ + + + + + D + + + + T B + +
+ + + + + + + E + + + E E + +
O V E R R E A C H E D A A + Y
D + E L B O N T + C + C C + T
U I + + + + R D + + A H H + I
+ N S + + O E + + + + E + + L
+ + A A U L + + + + + R R + I
+ + + B B + D E L B A S I D B
+ + L A L I + + + + + + + + A
+ E N + + E L + + + + B + + +
D E + + + + + I + + E + + + +
+ + + + + + + + T E + + + + +
+ + + + + + + + C Y + + + + +
+ + + + + + + H + + + + + + +
+ + P E A C H E S + + + + + +
```

Continued from Day 99

(Over,Down,Direction)
ABILITY(15,9,N)
BEACH(13,1,S)
BEECH(12,10,SW)
DISABILITY(1,4,SE)
DISABLED(14,8,W)
ENABLED(2,11,NE)

NOBLE(7,4,W)
OVERREACHED(1,3,E)
PEACHES(3,15,E)
REACHED(13,7,NW)
TEACHERS(12,1,S)
TROUBLED(8,4,SW)
UNABLE(1,5,SE)

Day 102
Fill in the blank:
1. My brother has several **scars** on his legs from football spikes.
2. Do you use a **charcoal** or gas grill?
3. My grandfather enjoyed smoking **cigars**.
4. How many cups in two **quarts**?
5. The spring sports **awards** ceremony is next week.
6. That sculpture really **dwarfs** the other ones.
7. How many **quarters** are there in a dollar?
8. While we were hiking, we dodged several **swarms** of bees.
9. **Zanzibar** is part of Tanzania.
10. He is a true **superstar**.

Day 103
Unscramble these
1. setrrad **starred**
2. rdscear **scarred**
3. drrsaep **sparred**
4. erchrad **charred**
5. werard **warred**
6. zqruat **quartz**
7. rueesolraqm **quarrelsome**
8. readadw **awarded**
9. warrtnead **warranted**
10. hrsvawe **wharves**

Day 105
Fill in the blank
1. I can't even remember how the **quarrel** started.
2. Each **notch** on the belt represents a win.
3. The ink made a permanent **blotch** on the paper.
4. Don't be **such** a sourpuss!
5. Her gentle **touch** was very soothing.
6. We asked the **butcher** to cut us some steaks for dinner.
7. Did you **watch** the ballgame last night?
8. Lisa used the fly **swatter** to **swat** the fly.
9. A **kumquat** is an exotic fruit.
10. Jake, our bulldog, is a good **watchdog**.

Day 107

1. lrudarqee **quarreled**
2. qriuared **quarried**
3. ncsuoi **cousin**
4. tohducere **retouched**
5. utyoch **touchy**
6. etcwhda **watched**
7. bthceurde **butchered**
8. qsetdtua **squatted**
9. edtwsat **swatted**
10. vsuae **suave**

Day 108

```
+ + C + + + + + + + + S + Q T +
H C T O N P O T W + E + U H +
+ + + + U + + A + G H + A G +
+ + + G + S T + N + C + L I +
+ + + + N C I I + + T + I T +
+ + + + H I L N + + U + T R +
W + + M + E H + S + R + Y E +
+ A E + R + + C + + C + + T W
+ N T R S Q U A T T E R S A A
+ + A E + + + + + O + + + W T
+ U + + R + + + + + B + + + C
Q + + + + M E Q U A L I T Y H
+ + + + + + + A + + + + + + I
+ + + + + + + + R + + + + + N
+ + + + + + + + K + + + + + G
```

(Over,Down,Direction)

BOTCHING(11,11,NW)   SQUATTERS(5,9,E)
COUSINS(3,1,SE)   TOPNOTCH(8,2,W)
CRUTCHES(11,8,N)   WATCHING(15,8,S)
EQUALITY(7,12,E)   WATCHMEN(9,2,SW)
QUALITY(13,1,S)   WATERMARK(1,7,SE)
QUARRELING(1,12,NE)   WATERTIGHT(14,10,N)

Day 115

Fill in the blank

1. My mom and dad **met** at the beach.
2. Babies don't like to eat **beets**.
3. Looking out the window at the storm, Jessica **sighed** heavily.
4. That clap of thunder **frightened** me.
5. I **tightened** my seatbelt before the plane took off.
6. Taking some books out of my backpack **lightened** it.
7. What are you two **fighting** about?
8. Mount Blanc is one of the **highest** peaks in the Alps.
9. She walked so **lightly** I didn't hear her come in.
10. We had such a **delightful** time yesterday.

Day 116

```
S T E E K A R A P + + I + + G
+ + + Y R I G H T I N G + + N
+ + + + L + + + + D + + + + I
Y L L U F T H G I L E D S B N
G + T + S + H S + N + K R U T
+ N + I + I C G O + N + E L H
+ + I + G R G I I I + S N L G
+ + + N E H T H G S G + E F I
+ + + T E E T H I N N + T I L
+ + I + R T T E I N + U E G +
+ O + C + H H T N + G + E H +
N + S + O + E G + I + + W T +
+ I + O + E + + + I + N S S +
D + D + M + + + + R + G + + +
L I G H T E N I N G F + + + +
```

(Over,Down,Direction)

BULLFIGHTS(14,4,S)   LIGHTNING(15,9,N)
DELIGHTFULLY(12,4,W)   MEETINGS(5,14,NE)
DISCRETION(1,14,NE)   PARAKEETS(9,1,W)
FRIGHTENING(11,15,NW)   RIGHTING(5,2,E)
INDISCRETION(12,1,SW)   SIGHING(5,5,SE)
KNIGHTHOOD(12,5,SW)   SWEETENERS(13,13,N)
LIGHTENING(1,15,E)   TIGHTENING(3,5,SE)
                          UNSIGHTLY(12,10,NW)

Day 119

Fill in the blank:

1. You **ought not** do that.
2. Thank you! That was so **thoughtful**!
3. Lisa **thoughtfully** asked if Emma needed help.
4. Uncle Jack has a hearty **laugh**.
5. Adam **caught** Sam's fly ball.
6. He is an **honest** man.
7. Tom is so **friendly**.
8. I **spent** too much money at the store today.
9. Did you get the letter I **sent** last week?
10. Bill **lent** Brian his pencil.

Day 122

1. mrdoeeendmc **recommended**
2. mdnse **mends**
3. nmdecmso **commends**
4. enchrpmeoedd **comprehended**
5. dnspeed **depends**
6. ednst **tends**
7. edtredvoexne **overextended**
8. tnesdopr **portends**
9. nsdsiedt **distends**
10. idiendvsd **dividends**

Day 125

Fill in the blank:

1. I don't have **any** clean clothes.
2. Do you know **anything** about this?
3. A tadpole is a **tiny** relative of a frog.
4. Brad found a **shiny** new penny.
5. Mr. Wilson was my dad's favorite **crony**.
6. That idea seems a little **loony**.
7. We sat in the **balcony** for the **ceremony**.
8. The police have him under **scrutiny**.
9. She will give her **testimony** in court on Wednesday.
10. There will be a **mutiny** if summer vacation is canceled.

Day 126

1. yoybdna **anybody**
2. eitrbsnia **brainiest**
3. nsttiei **tiniest**
4. oreacnlime **ceremonial**
5. inoiaalmrtm **matrimonial**
6. infryetrta **fraternity**
7. oiotyrrs **sorority**
8. teatetsmn **testament**
9. inattiesond **destination**
10. neeopsi **peonies**

Day 130

1. okooeevldr **overlooked**
2. ospkbcrao **scrapbook**
3. kokeoibngep **bookkeeping**
4. fofolproo **foolproof**
5. fogode **goofed**
6. opsofr **proofs**
7. kssoop **spooks**
8. vahlse **halves**
9. rkosob **brooks**
10. olfsk **folks**

Day 131

Fill in the blank

1. Wow! Jack was really acting **goofy** today.
2. It helps to have **waterproof** boots when you go fly fishing.
3. We scrambled to get out of the way of the horses' hooves.
4. What **spooked** the cat?
5. **It's too hot** to touch.
6. Look at that double **yolk** egg!
7. Purse is another name for a **pocketbook**.
8. My brother is a **rookie** firefighter.
9. Please put the **yearbooks** on that **bookshelf**.

Day 132

```
+ L + G + + C + T + B T P K L
H + A + N O + S + O + A + O O
+ A + U O I E + O + S M + O O
G + L K G I V K + S + P + B K
N + I V F H S O B + + E + E I
I E S O I H T O R + + R + D N
F + O K E N O E + P + P + I G
A G + L O K G + R + + R + U L
O + V F O O R P D N U O S G A
L E + K O O B K O O C O + + U
S + + + + + + H + + + F + + G
S P O O F I N G C + + + + + H
R O O K I E S + + T + + + + I
+ + + + + + + + + + A + + + N
+ + + + + + + + + + M + + G
```

(Over, Down, Direction)

BOOKSHELVES(11,1,SW)	LOAFING(1,10,N)
COOKBOOK(11,10,W)	LOOKING(15,1,S)
COOKIE(7,1,SW)	MATCHBOOKS(12,15,NW)
GOOFIEST(2,8,NE)	PASSBOOK(13,1,SW)
GUIDEBOOK(14,9,N)	PROVING(10,7,NW)
HALVING(1,2,SE)	ROOKIES(1,13,E)
LAUGHING(15,8,S)	SOUNDPROOF(13,9,W)
LAUGHTER(2,1,SE)	SPOOFING(1,12,E)
	TAMPERPROOF(12,1,S)

Day 135

Fill in the blank

1. To row a boat, you need to have oars in the **oarlock**.
2. The eagle **soared** high over the treetops.
3. **Although** we won the game, we were still upset with the officiating.
4. Horses are used for transportation **throughout** the world.
5. My sister got **married** last Saturday.
6. Lisa's eyes danced with **merriment**.
7. Have you ever tasted a **thimbleberry**?
8. The accident **occurred** on an icy road.
9. We **carried** the boxes to the curb.
10. My aunt got her fur coat from a **furrier**.

Day 139

1. bhiigdnumrm **hummingbird**
2. velbra **verbal**
3. eabrlh **herbal**
4. oedrwfdra **forwarded**
5. ourrndcce **concurred**
6. peobrrv **proverb**
7. mrudemru **murmured**
8. bcdwaark **backward**
9. wdscroa **cowards**
10. eerdbda **bearded**

       Sequential Spelling Level 3 - Teacher's Guide

Day 141
Fill in the blank:
1. She's a great **hurdler** for a **girl**.
2. Flamenco skirts **swirl** prettily.
3. The police officer was very **firm** in dealing with the crowd.
4. I called to **confirm** our reservations for next Tuesday.
5. My little sister started to **squirm** halfway through dinner.
6. The doctor called to **inform** us that the test was negative.
7. He's going to **perform** at the comedy club on Thursday night.
8. Two cars per family are now the **norm** in most suburbs.
9. I didn't mean to **misinform** you.
10. Using a **whirlpool** helps people with arthritis.

Day 142
Unscramble these
1. wndirwhli **whirlwind**
2. msrtafnsor **transforms**
3. efoprsmr **performs**
4. fomcrsno **conforms**
5. rheludsr **hurdlers**
6. fmoaverit **formative**
7. nouisrmf **uniforms**
8. miffasr **affirms**
9. swlisr **swirls**
10. rstilw **twirls**

Day 144
```
N + + + F + W H I R L I N G E
+ O + + + O + + + + S O + + V
+ C I + + + R + + Q I + + + I
+ O + T + + + M U T + + + + T
+ N + + A + + I A + + + + + A
+ F + + + M R M + T + + + + M
N O I T A M R O F N I S I M R
A R + + I O + I G + + O + + I
B M + N F + + N F + + + N + F
S I G N + + I + + N + + + S F
U T I + + L + + + + O + + + A
R Y N O R M A L I T Y C + + +
D + + I P E R F O R M A N C E
L + W + + + + G N I L D R U C
Y T + Y T I M R O F E D + + +
```

(Over,Down,Direction)
ABSURDLY(1,8,S)
AFFIRMATIVE(15,11,N)
CONFIRMATION(12,12,NW)
CONFORMITY(2,3,S)
CURDLING(15,14,W)
DEFORMITY(12,15,W)
FORMATIONS(5,1,SE)
INFORMATION(3,11,NE)
MISINFORMATION(14,7,W)
NORMALITY(3,12,E)
PERFORMANCE(5,13,E)
SQUIRMING(11,2,SW)
TWIRLING(2,15,NE)
WHIRLING(7,1,E)

Day 146
Fill in the blank
1. On a visit to the museum, we saw lots of old **harnesses**.
2. Everyone **learns** differently.
3. Do you know how much money a doctor **earns**?
4. We need to take these to the **returns** desk.
5. Lisa and Emily both got **sunburns** at the beach last week.
6. I don't like to eat **turnips**, but my dad does.
7. We take our knives to Mr. Sullivan, who **sharpens** them for us.
8. Jake ran the vacuum over the **carpets** before his mom got home.
9. At an early age, children learn to take **turns** with their toys.
10. We need to remember to pack the **tarps** before we go camping.

Day 151
Unscramble these
1. wdarpe **warped**
2. chrdeip **chirped**
3. rashlma **marshal**
4. dodlsbuseeorc **doublecrossed**
5. lsesodg **glossed**
6. erdenestit **interested**
7. ocrrgse **grocers**
8. rieihssttt **thirstiest**
9. leuppr **purple**
10. aswamollmrh **marshmallow**

Day 155
Unscramble these
1. adeotcs **coasted**
2. trosdea **roasted**
3. uliipft **pitiful**
4. buetuafil **beautiful**
5. csateor **coaster**
6. aesrrto **roaster**
7. educl **clued**
8. ydTseaus **Tuesdays**
9. toulghha **although**
10. pusutri **pursuit**

Day 156

```
S  T  I  U  S  R  U  P  G  G  +  +  T  S  +
+  +  +  +  +  +  +  N  +  N  +  +  H  U  +
+  +  +  +  +  +  I  +  +  I  +  +  O  I  +
+  +  +  +  +  T  +  +  +  Y  +  +  R  N  +
Y  R  O  A  S  T  I  N  G  T  +  +  O  G  +
L  +  +  A  Y  +  +  +  +  I  +  +  U  +  +
L  +  O  +  +  L  B  A  +  +  P  +  +  +  +
U  C  +  +  S  +  L  O  V  +  +  +  H  +  +
F  +  +  +  +  R  +  U  A  E  +  +  +  +  +
I  +  +  +  +  E  +  F  S  N  +  +  +  +  +
T  +  +  Y  L  L  U  F  I  T  U  A  E  B
U  T  H  R  O  U  G  H  S  +  T  I  E  +  +
D  +  +  +  +  +  +  +  +  R  +  I  N  +  +
+  +  +  +  +  +  +  +  +  +  U  +  P  G  +
+  +  +  +  +  +  +  +  +  +  +  P  +  +  +
```

(Over, Down, Direction)

AVENUE(8,7,SE)	PITYING(10,7,N)
BEAUTIFULLY(15,11,W)	PURSUERS(12,15,NW)
BOASTING(7,7,SE)	PURSUITS(8,1,W)
COASTING(2,8,NE)	ROASTING(2,5,E)
DUTIFULLY(1,13,N)	SUING(14,1,S)
PITIFULLY(13,14,NW)	THOROUGH(13,1,S)
	THROUGH(2,12,E)

Day 159

Fill in the blank

1. The lawyer **argued** his case before the Supreme Court.
2. After being **rescued**, we thanked our **rescuer**.
3. I wanted to replace the torn wallpaper, but the pattern was **discontinued** last year.
4. The antique desk was **valued** at over twenty thousand dollars.
5. The **continual** blaring of the siren was very annoying.
6. We drove **through** the Rockies on the way to Seattle.
7. Brian **studied** the chess board before moving his pawn.
8. Although she's still a full-time **student**, she is looking forward to graduation.
9. Do you think the apartment will be **suitable** for all four of us?
10. **Nobody** thought that would happen.

Day 162

Fill in the blank:

1. Your decision **saddens** me.
2. Do you know which door this key **opens**?
3. What's the **worst** that could happen?
4. Let's wait and see what **happens**.
5. The light from the lamp really **brightens** the room.
6. I'm glad to know someone **listens** to me.
7. Flour **thickens** gravy.
8. Sugar **sweetens** iced tea.
9. What fabric **softeners** do you use?
10. Look at how the snow **glistens** in the sunlight!

Day 163

Unscramble these

1. adseddne **saddened**
2. ponede **opened**
3. desnoelo **loosened**
4. dhtegient **tightened**
5. rndheattee **threatened**
6. dnsletei **listened**
7. tedsaenf **fastened**
8. sroew **worse**
9. ehsitgenatdr **straightened**
10. eetosndf **softened**

Day 168

```
F  +  +  +  S  G  P  +  +  +  +  +  S  B  S
I  +  +  +  T  O  N  I  +  +  +  T  U  +  T
D  +  +  +  E  +  +  I  C  +  E  F  +  +  E
G  +  +  M  G  +  +  +  T  K  F  +  G  +  K
E  +  S  +  D  +  +  +  N  E  E  N  +  +  C
T  +  +  +  U  +  +  U  T  +  I  T  +  +  U
I  +  +  +  B  +  J  I  +  T  +  U  I  +  B
N  +  +  +  S  +  N  +  E  +  +  +  Q  N  +
G  +  +  +  S  +  G  +  K  +  +  +  +  +  +
P  O  +  +  U  +  N  S  T  E  K  C  I  H  T
O  +  B  +  F  A  M  A  R  K  E  T  I  N  G
E  +  +  L  L  B  U  F  F  E  T  +  +  +  +
T  +  +  B  E  +  +  +  +  +  +  +  +  +  +
I  +  +  +  +  T  +  +  +  +  +  +  +  +  +
C  +  +  +  +  +  +  +  +  +  +  +  +  +  +
```

(Over,Down,Direction)

BLANKETING(4,13,NE)	JUNKETS(7,7,NE)
BUCKETS(15,7,N)	MARKETING(7,11,E)
BUFFET(6,12,E)	PICKETING(7,1,SE)
BUFFETING(14,1,SW)	POEMS(7,1,SW)
FIDGETING(1,1,S)	POETIC(1,10,S)
FUSSBUDGETS(5,11,N)	QUIETING(13,8,NW)
GOBLET(1,9,SE)	THICKETS(15,10,W)

Day 169

Fill in the blank:

1. Saturn is a **planet** with rings around it.
2. We went shopping for new **carpet** yesterday.
3. If we take a trip to Japan, we're going to need an **interpreter** to **interpret** the signs.
4. Please hang your coat in the **closet**.
5. I took my tennis **racket** to the **Racquet** Club.
6. Would you like to attend the **banquet** with me?
7. Janet makes a great mushroom **omelet**.
8. What a pretty **bracelet**!
9. There is information about that painting in this **pamphlet**.
10. We paddled the canoe to the **inlet** and had a picnic.

Day 170

Unscramble these
1. lteoosbk **booklets**
2. cstlseo **closets**
3. belulst **bullets**
4. tprriteeresn **interpreters**
5. vneveetel **velveteen**
6. letabrecs **bracelets**
7. psempatlh **pamphlets**
8. seltapn **planets**
9. stmcoe **comets**
10. evtlsoi **violets**

Day 175

1. lrsmbuegr **grumblers**
2. utogbh **bought**
3. uttgfholuh **thoughtful**
4. lhgyrtuoho **thoroughly**
5. ssccsufule **successful**
6. sspnorfieo **profession**
7. drpnioeess **depression**
8. bereeemdmr **remembered**
9. ipgpikns **skipping**
10. ptudicer **pictured**

Day 176

```
S+  G  +  T  S  H  G  U  A  L  L  +  R  +
DS  +  N  +  H  +  +  G  +  A  C  Y  E  +
+I  E  +  I  +  R  N  +  N  +  R  L  M  +
++  S  N  +  L  I  O  O  +  +  U  L  E  S
++  +  C  H  R  B  I  U  +  +  S  U  M  E
++  +  +  U  G  S  M  +  G  +  H  F  B  H
++  +  T  +  S  U  +  U  +  H  E  S  E  C
++  C  +  E  +  S  O  +  R  +  S  S  R  T
+E  +  F  +  +  +  I  R  +  G  +  E  I  E
L+  O  +  +  +  +  +  O  O  +  +  C  N  R
+R  +  +  +  +  +  +  N  H  +  C  G  T
PG  N  I  D  E  E  C  C  U  S  T  U  +  S
DE  P  R  E  S  S  I  O  N  S  +  S  +  +
++  +  +  +  S  P  L  A  S  H  E  S  +  +
SS  E  N  L  U  F  T  H  G  U  O  H  T  +
```

(Over,Down,Direction)
CRUSHES(12,2,S)
DEPRESSIONS(1,13,E)
DISCUSSIONS(1,2,SE)
GRUMBLING(11,9,NW)
LAUGHS(11,1,W)
LECTURING(1,10,NE)
PROFESSIONAL(1,12,NE)
REMEMBERING(14,1,S)
SPLASHES(6,14,E)
STRETCHES(15,12,N)
SUCCEEDING(11,12,W)
SUCCESSFULLY(13,13,N)
THOROUGHNESS(12,12,NW)
THOUGHTFULNESS(14,15,W)
THROUGH(5,1,SE)

Day 179

Fill in the blank:
1. If you speed in a construction zone, the fine is **doubled**.
2. I am **troubled** by her decision to leave.
3. Jack was **awarded** his varsity letter for baseball.
4. The evidence **proved** his guilt.
5. Sam's mom had a tumor **removed** yesterday.
6. It **occurred** to me that I had forgotten her birthday.
7. The board **approved** the hiring of an executive director.
8. That's the **corniest** joke I've ever heard!
9. Our neighbors are very **friendly**.
10. We're planning a **barbecue** this summer.

Frequently Recurring Spelling Rules

FLOSS RULE

A one-syllable base word with one short vowel immediately before the final sounds of (f), (l), or (s) is spelled with ff, ll, or ss.

Examples:

off

ball

miss

Exceptions to this rule: yes, gas, bus, plus, this

RABBIT RULE

Double the consonants b, d, g, m, n and p after a short vowel in a two syllable word.

Examples:

rabbit

manner

dagger

banner

drummer

DOUBLING RULE

A base word ending in one consonant after an accented short vowel doubles the final consonant before a suffix beginning with a vowel.

Examples:

run + ing = running

stop + ed = stopped

hop+ ing = hopping

DROPPING RULE

A base word ending in silent "e" drops "e" before a suffix beginning with a vowel.

Examples.

hope + ing = hoping

shine + ing = shining

slope + ed = sloped

CHANGING RULE

A base word ending in "y" after a consonant changes "y" to "i" before any suffix (except one beginning with "i").

Examples:

baby + ies = babies

lady + ies = ladies

boy + s = boys

toy +s = toys

Remember: You change the babies not the boys!